The Truth

Student's Book

Book 2

The Way, the Truth and the Life series
Religious Education series for 11 to 14 year olds

Key Stage 3

Contributors: Ged Clapson, Mary O'Grady, Therese Piper

CATHOLIC TRUTH SOCIETY
PUBLISHERS TO THE HOLY SEE

The Truth - Student's Book

Nihil obstat: Father Anton Cowan (Censor)
Imprimatur: Monsignor Thomas Egan, V.G., Westminster, 1st November 2000, Feast of All Saints
The Nihil obstat and Imprimatur *are a declaration that the book or pamphlet is considered to be free from doctrinal or moral error. It is not implied that those who have granted the* Nihil obstat *and* Imprimatur *agree with the contents, opinions or statements expressed.*

© 2001 The Incorporated Catholic Truth Society.

Published 2001 by The Incorporated Catholic Truth Society, 40-46 Harleyford Road, London SE11 5AY
Tel: 020 7640 0042 Fax: 020 7640 0046

ISBN: 978 1 86082 101 1 CTS Code: Ed 08

Designed and Produced by: The Catholic Truth Society/ Stephen Campbell.

Picture Research: The Catholic Truth Society/ Pierpaolo Finaldi.

Illustrations: © Dave Bowyer, © Darrell Warner, © Dave Thompson. All illustrators co-ordinated by Paul Beebee/ Beehive Illustration Agency.

Printed by: Printhaus.

The publisher acknowledges permission to reproduce the following:- Cover: Noli Me Tangere, 1442 (fresco) by Fra Angelico (Guido di Pietro) (c.1387-1455) Museo di San Marco dell'Angelico, Florence, Italy/Bridgeman Art Library, Palm Sunday Procession in Jerusalem © PA News, Boy carrying cross in Holy Week Via Dolorosa Procession © ASAP Israel Images, Missionaries of Charity Sister holding boy and olive branch © PA News. © Andes Press Agency / Carlos Reyes-Manzo pages 16,21,41,42,55,58,69,70,72,74,77 Page 7: © Adam Woolfitt/CORBIS, © Douglas Peebles/CORBIS. Page 8: © Historical Picture Archive/CORBIS. Page 9: © Stephen Campbell. Page 10: Digital Imagery© copyright 2000 PhotoDisc, Inc. Page 11: © Kevin R. Morris/CORBIS, Scientist. Page 13: © Danny Lehman/CORBIS, © Lennart Nilsson, A CHILD IS BORN/Albert Bonniers Förlag. Page 14: Digital Imagery© copyright 2000 PhotoDisc, Inc. Page 16: © Leonard de Selva/CORBIS, The Temptation of Adam and Eve (details of the heads of Adam and Eve), c.1427 (fresco) by Tommaso Masolino (1383-1447) Brancacci Chapel, Santa Maria del Carmine, Florence, Italy/Bridgeman Art Library. Page 17: © Jennie Woodcock; Reflections Photolibrary/CORBIS. Page 18: © Tony Arruza/CORBIS, © Lawson Wood/CORBIS. Page 19: © Kevin Schafer/CORBIS, © Roger Ressmeyer/CORBIS, © Alan Towse; Ecoscene/CORBIS, © Wolfgan Kaehler/CORBIS, © Bill Varie/CORBIS. Page 23: © Craig Aurness/CORBIS. Page 24 © WildCountry/CORBIS. Page 25: Abraham and Isaac (detail) by Ferdinand Olivier, Courtesy of the Trustees, The National Gallery, London. Page 26: © Bettmann/CORBIS. Page 33: © Candle Books, London. Page 34: © ASAP/Israel Images, © Roger Ressmeyer/CORBIS. Page 35: © Shelley Gazin/CORBIS. Page 37: © O. Alamany & E. Vicen/CORBIS. Page 41: Abraham and the Three Angels, icon (tempera on panel), from Macedonia, c. 1700, Greek School Richardson and Kailas Icons, London/Bridgeman. Page 43: © PA News. Page 45: © ASAP Israel Images, © Bettmann/Corbis, © Arte e Immagini srl/CORBIS, © Archivio Iconografico, S.A./CORBIS. Page 46: © Candle Books, London. Page 47: © ASAP Israel Images. Page 50: Caravaggio, The Taking of Christ (1602), with kind permission of the Jesuit community who acknowledge the generosity of Dr. Marie Lee Wilson. Page 51: © ASAP Israel Images. Page 53: Ecce Homo, c.1625-26 by Sir Anthony van Dyck (1599-1641) The Barber Institute of Fine Arts, University of Birmingham/Bridgeman Art Library, What is Truth? (Christ and Pilate) 1890 (oil on canvas) by Ge (Gay), Nikolai Nikolaevich (1831-94) Gallery, Moscow, Russia/Bridgeman Art Library. Page 54: © PA News, The Way to Calvary (detail) by Jacopo Bassano courtesy of the Trustees, The National Gallery, London. Christ of St John of the Cross, 1951 (oil on canvas) by Salvador Dali (1904-89) Glasgow Art Gallery and Museum, Scotland/Bridgeman Art Library. Page 57: © Ted Spiegel/CORBIS. Page 60: The Incredulity of St Thomas (detail) Guercino, courtesy of the Trustees, The National Gallery, London. Page 63: The Prophet Isaiah by Pietro Perugino (c.1445-1523) Musee des Beaux-Arts, Nantes, France/Bridgeman Art Library. Page 68: © PA News. Page 71: © Jim Holmes/CAFOD. Page 74: © Sergio Dorantes/CORBIS. Page 75: © Servizio Fotografico de L'Osservatore Romano. Page 76: © Bettmann/CORBIS, Courtesy of the Marquette University Archives. Page 79: Roundel from Roman Villa, Hinton St Mary, Dorset (mosaic) by Roman (4th century AD) Dorset County Museum, UK/Bridgeman Art Library. Page 82: © Holy Transfiguration Monastery, MA USA. Page 83: © Phil Sayer, © Bettmann/CORBIS. Page 84: King Henry VIII by Unknown Artist, Catherine of Aragon by Unknown Artist, Anne Boleyn by Unknown Artist, By Courtesy of the National Portrait Gallery, London. Page 85: Sir Thomas More by Unknown Artist, John Fisher by Unknown Artist, © Jonathan Blair/CORBIS. Page 67: Edward VI by Unknown Artist, By Courtesy of the National Portrait Gallery, London. Page 88: Mary I by Master John, Elizabeth I by Unknown Artist, By Courtesy of the National Portrait Gallery, London. Page 89: © Beda College, Rome, Edmund Campion by J. Neefs By Courtesy of the National Portrait Gallery, London. Page 92: Cardinal John Henry Newman by Sir John Everett Millais, By Courtesy of the National Portrait Gallery, London. Page 93: Cardinal Nicholas Patrick Stephen Wiseman, attributed to Henry Edward Doyle By Courtesy of the National Portrait Gallery, London. Page 95: © Bettmann/CORBIS. Page 96: © PA News. Page 97: © Hulton Getty. (For those images for which we have been unable to trace the copyright holder, the Publisher would be grateful to receive any information as to their identity).

Introduction

Welcome to 'The Way, the Truth and the Life' series. It is Jesus who said: 'I am the Way, the Truth and the Life' - *John 14:6*. This is one of the most important statements of Jesus and an invitation to each of us into a journey of great discovery.

As you progress through your RE lessons in Key Stage 3, I hope you will come to appreciate more deeply everything that God wants to teach us through his revelation in Jesus Christ. We meet Christ both in the words of the Scriptures and in the teaching of the Church. You are going to study both.

This book will open up for you the Truth. What God gives us is the Truth both about yourselves and about God's own life. So these are very important truths that you will be studying. But they are more than cold truths. They are the truths for the heart and they will lead us into the fullness of life.

✠ Vincent Nichols
Archbishop of Birmingham, November 2000.

The Truth - Student's Book

Contents

Introduction 3	The Story of Exodus and
Contents 4	the Passover 26
Acknowledgements 6	Who was Moses? 27
1. Creation 7	God Speaks to Moses 29
In the Beginning 7	The Passover 31
The Creation Story in Genesis 8	The Passover Today 34
The Creation 9	The Ten Commandments 36
Truth 11	Jesus: The New Covenant 38
God is Creator and Sustainer 12	3. Exploring the Mass 41
In God's Image and Likeness 13	4. The Paschal Mystery 43
Made in God's Own Image . . . 15	Travelling with Jesus 43
God's Great Love 16	Holy Week 45
Stewards of the Earth 18	Palm Sunday 46
Is it too late? 19	The Last Supper 48
The End of Paradise... But still a Promise 20	The Garden of Gethsemane . . 50
	The Trial Before the Sanhedrin 51
	The Trial Before Pilate 53
2. Covenant 21	The Way of the Cross 54
Promises 21	The Death of Jesus 56
The First Covenant 23	Holy Saturday 58
God's Covenant with Abraham 24	The Resurrection 60
	The Paschal Mystery 62

Contents

5. The Prophetic Role of the Church 63

God's message proclaimed by the Prophets 64

Jesus fulfils the Old Testament Prophecies 67

Being a Follower of Jesus ... 68

Go out to the World 70

The Church's Teaching 72

Modern Day Prophets 74

John Paul II 74

Mother Teresa 74

Jean Vanier 75

Dorothy Day 76

Archbishop Oscar Romero ... 77

6. The Church in Britain 79

The First British Martyr 80

The First Missionaries 82

A Christian Nation 83

How present day divisions among Christians arose 84

The Reformation in England and Wales 87

Emancipation 92

Christians Divided 94

The Second Vatican Council . 95

Glossary 99

Acknowledgements

Considerable thanks are due to all the RE teachers of the secondary schools in the North and East Areas of the Westminster Archdiocese who contributed to this Student's Book by way of advice, editorial review and comment. *'The Way, the Truth and the Life'* series for Key Stage 3 Religious Education has been a collaborative exercise from start to finish. Kind thanks are expressed in particular to the following schools:

(East area, Westminster Archdiocese:)
Bishop Challoner RC School, Tower Hamlets.
Blessed John Roche RC School, Tower Hamlets.
Cardinal Pole RC School, Hackney.
La Sainte Union Convent School, Camden.
Mount Carmel RC Technology College for Girls School, Islington.
Maria Fidelis Convent School, Camden.
St. Aloysius College, Islington.

(North area, Westminster Archdiocese)
Bishop Douglas RC School, Barnet.
Cardinal Hinsley RC High School, Brent.
Convent of Jesus & Mary Language College, Brent.
Finchley Catholic High School, Barnet.
St. Gregory's RC School, Brent.
St. Michael's Grammar School, Barnet.
St. Anne's RC School, Enfield.
St. James' RC High School, Barnet.
St. Thomas More RC School, Haringey.
St. Martha's Convent School, Barnet.
Salvatorian College, Harrow.
St. Ignatius College, Enfield.
Sacred Heart RC School, Harrow.

Sr. Marcellina Cooney, CP, Secondary RE Adviser of the North and East Areas of Westminster Archdiocese has co-ordinated this project throughout, and Rt. Rev. Vincent Nichols, as Bishop in North London, supported and encouraged this project since its earliest beginnings.

The supporting website http://www.tere.org was set up thanks to the partnership between Mount Carmel Roman Catholic School for Girls (London Borough of Islington) and City and Islington College. Design was by Tamarin Design Ltd.

Worksheets have been developed in conjunction with this Student's Book for classroom use, and are to be found in the companion Teacher's Book. Schools using this Student's Book should also take full advantage of the Teacher's Book and the supporting Web site. Essential teaching and classroom materials directly linked to this Student's Book are available in a sister publication 'Exploring the Mass' (Teacher's Book, Student's Book and Video), published by CTS.

1 Creation

In the Beginning

Close your eyes and sit in total silence. Concentrate on the experience - not on the darkness, but on the 'nothingness' of it. Imagine there is nothing around you at all: even *you* do not exist. There is nothing to see, to hear, to taste, to smell or to feel. Nothing exists: no stars, no earth, no wildlife, no air, no water, and no human beings. This is perhaps as close to understanding pre-Creation as we can get.

"There was darkness over the deep and God's spirit hovered over the water." (Gen 1:2)

Now open your eyes. This is like the moment when God said: "Let there be light!" Look around and carefully study everything you see. Look beyond what things are now and think about where they really came from. A desk is not a desk, but wood that came from a tree, crafted by a carpenter. A shirt is made from cotton grown on a plant in a distant country. A light bulb is a combination of glass made from sand, and metal which glows when electricity is applied to it. What else can you see?

The people of the Old Testament wanted to know about the Creation of the universe. In order to help their readers to understand the mysterious action of God, the writers of Genesis used symbolic stories to get across important truths. The important messages in the stories of Creation are:

- that nothing exists which does not owe its existence to God the Creator;

- because God is infinitely good, Creation reflects his goodness;

- God created humankind in his own image and likeness;

- God made humankind the stewards of Creation.

"Let the heavens be glad, let earth rejoice, let the sea thunder and all that it holds..." (Psalm 96:1)

Glossary
PRE-CREATION, CREATION, SYMBOLIC, IMAGE AND LIKENESS, STEWARD.

Creation

The Creation Story in Genesis

Activities

1. In the box below are six references from the Bible story of Creation.

Look them up and write out each verse:

> Gen. 1:1, Gen. 1:31, Gen. 1:28, Gen. 1:26, Gen. 2:18, Gen. 2:7.

2. In the table below there are twelve statements. Find six that best explain the meaning of the Genesis Creation story. Then match each one with the appropriate Bible reference above.

(a) God wants human beings to live in relationship with one another.

(b) God wants people to fill the earth and be masters of it.

(c) God became a human being in Jesus and lived among us.

(d) Because the world was made by God, it is good.

(e) Human beings are made to have a relationship with God.

(f) God made human beings like himself and gave us free will; therefore, we can choose to do whatever we like.

(g) The greatest of God's commandments is to love God and love your neighbour as you love yourself.

(h) God has given human beings the job of looking after his Creation.

(i) Everything that exists was made by God.

(j) God chose the people of Israel to be his own people.

(k) The world belongs to human beings to do what they want with it.

(l) God gives people his own breath of life.

3. Look at the six Bible quotations and the six statements you have selected.

Choose three of them. For each one explain:

(i) how it should affect the way we live and behave today;

(ii) how *you* could put it into practice in your own everyday life.

Extension

Many cultures have their own Creation stories. Can you find one of these? (The library would be a good starting point.) Describe this Creation story. What similarities are there to the story in Genesis, what differences? What does it tell us about the people who wrote the story?

Brahma, the Hindu God of Creation.

The Creation

Dr. Knowit says...

"The story of Creation is a fairy tale for children. We're grown up now. We know that the big bang started the world. We know it was sheer chance over billions of years that led to a planet like ours. Life developed and became more complex over more billions of years. This happened by a process called evolution. The story of the six-day-Creation is like the story of Santa Claus: a myth to grow out of."

Mr. Readit says...

"The Book of Genesis states quite clearly that God created the universe in six days and on the seventh day he sat back and admired it. There is no way in which God can lie, so all that is written in Genesis is absolutely true. We all know that the human race started with Adam and Eve who had lots of children and so the population grew."

Miss Bleevit says...

"I go along with both of you, but not totally. Let me explain. The truths contained in the Book of Genesis are **'theological truths'** - not **'scientific truths'**. They help explain our relationship with God, with our environment and with each other. We might not believe, these days, that the world was actually created in six days, but we do believe God created it over a period of time and that he loves us."

Activities

1. Explain how people who believe in God understand the story of Creation.

2. Explain how scientists understand the story of Creation.

3. Is it possible to be a scientist and believe in God at the same time? How does such a person understand the story of Creation?

4. In the story of Creation in Genesis:

(a) What is similar to our scientific knowledge of life and the universe?

(b) What is different from our scientific knowledge of life and the universe?

Creation

Research

5. Choose a tree, plant, flower or leaf.

(a) Describe in a scientific way how it has come into existence.

Scientific representation of a leaf.

(b) Describe in a poetic way how it came to be.

Poetic representation of leaves.

6. What does the Catholic Church teach about the creation of the universe?

To answer this question you will need to read the **Catechism of the Catholic Church**, paragraphs 337-343.

Key points to remember

Genesis, the story of Creation, is true, but not in a scientific way.

It is a statement of faith about God's relationship with the world and everything in it.

It states clearly that:

- nothing exists which does not owe its existence to God the Creator;

- God acted with total freedom;

- God is infinitely good and Creation reflects that goodness;

- God created humankind in his own image and likeness;

- God made humankind the stewards of Creation.

Glossary
EVOLUTION, THEOLOGICAL TRUTHS, SCIENTIFIC TRUTHS.

Creation

Truth

There are different ways of looking at truth. They do not necessarily contradict each other. So there are:

Theological Truths - things we believe which rely on faith.

Scientific Truths - facts that can be proven scientifically.

Activities

1. Look at the list below. Decide which is Scientific Truth and which is Theological Truth.

Copy only the letter into your exercise book and put 'S' (for scientific) or 'T' (for theological) beside it to indicate your choice; for example: **(a) T**.

(a) God created the universe.

(b) Coal is the result of decaying trees, millions of years old.

(c) When water is frozen it becomes ice.

(d) God loves me.

(e) Light travels at 186,000 miles per second.

(f) Life is a gift from God.

(g) The universe started with the 'big bang'.

(h) Human beings are very special because they are made in the image of God.

(i) Humans are responsible for looking after the earth.

(j) Life on earth began 2.5 billion years ago.

2. Now write two of your own scientific and two theological truths into your exercise book.

3. Study the following statements. Select and copy into your exercise book the statements that are true and omit the ones that are not true.

Group your answers under the following headings

  (i) True statements from the Bible.

  (ii) True statements from science.

The Bible Says:

(a) When Creation took place, there was nothing; the next moment everything was there.

(b) In its original form, everything in Creation was good.

(c) Before Creation, God existed.

(d) Humans can do whatever they like to the world and everything in it.

(e) There is a balance in nature that can be disrupted.

(f) Humankind was the final stage in Creation, the fulfilment of God's plan.

Science Says:

(g) The universe evolved over billions of years.

(h) There are many things about the earth which we still cannot explain.

(i) God created the heavens and the earth.

(j) Life on earth might have started in the seas, followed by amphibians, reptiles, birds and mammals.

(k) By failing to care for the environment, the balance of nature can be easily disrupted.

(l) The universe started with the 'big bang'.

Glossary
FAITH.

Creation

God is Creator and Sustainer

Christians believe that everything which exists is totally dependent upon God's power. That power of Creation is expressed in the Book of Genesis in the words: "Let there be..." So in the same way, if God were to say: "Let something stop being...", it would cease to be. In other words, the whole of Creation and each one of us, depends wholly on God having created us and looking after us.

However, Creation was not a 'one-off' event. It is going on constantly, and the fact that we go on living depends upon God caring for us and sustaining us. This is why God is called both Creator and Sustainer.

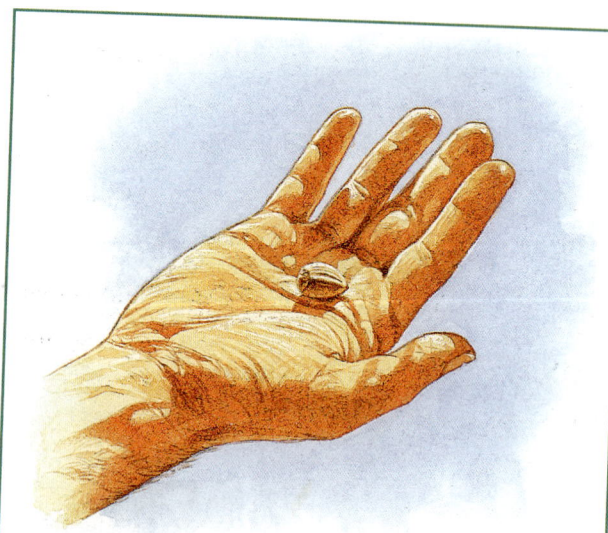

Julian of Norwich, a mystic, had a vision of God holding a very small thing in the palm of his hand. She asked God what it was that he was holding. God answered that it was everything that was created: 'God showed me a little thing, the size of a hazelnut lying in the palm of my hand. "What is this?" I thought. God replied, "It's everything I made." I looked at it: it seemed so small that it could break apart at any moment. "Don't worry," said God. "It will survive because I love it and look after it."'

Glossary
VISION, MYSTIC, SUSTAINER.

Activities

1. In what ways is God continuing to create and to look after our world?

2. Young children were asked where God was in this picture:

Sarah: *"In the sky looking down."*

Joel: *"In the sun because it gives life. Nothing could survive without the sun."*

Juanita: *"God is like the paper. You could have no drawing without the paper."*

(a) Discuss with the person beside you which answer you think is best. Write down this answer and explain why.

(b) What answer would you give if you were asked 'Where is God in this picture'?

Extension

3. "God does not create-to-forget, but creates and sustains (keeps in existence)."

Do you agree or disagree? Give reasons for your answer showing that you have considered more than one point of view.

Key points to remember

Christians believe:
- that God sustains everything that he has created.
- God's creative work has begun but has not ended.
- God does not abandon his Creation.

In God's Image and Likeness

According to the Book of Genesis, the last thing to be created was humankind - men and women. Read Genesis 1:26-31.

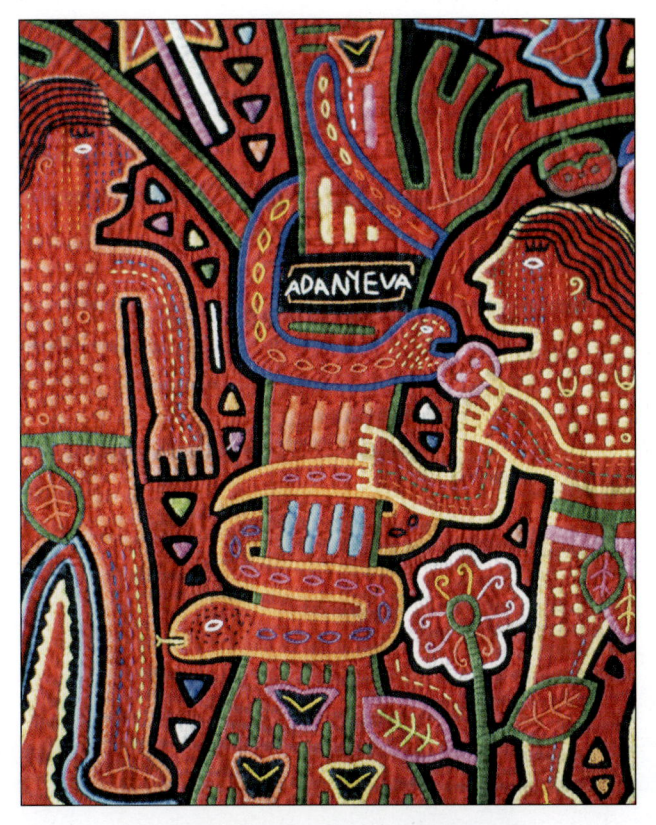

Adam and Eve tempted by the serpent.

The author of this account of Creation says that people are the most important part of Creation for God. That is why human beings are listed as the last things to be created. By being made 'in God's image and likeness', we are able to know and appreciate goodness. We are also able to develop the good in others and in Creation.

There are two stories of Creation in the Bible, written at different times by different people. They do not contradict each other; they just point out different things. The second story shows the special relationship between people and God. Human beings received life from God, and God wanted everything to be good and beautiful (like the Garden of Eden) for people.

The authors of the Creation stories wanted to explain the world around them and the place of human beings in it. Their stories contain Theological Truths, rather than Scientific Truths. One Theological Truth is that Adam and Eve represent humanity in its first state of goodness and holiness as created by God. However, by giving in to the tempter, Adam and Eve committed a personal sin. This sin, which is called 'original sin', has affected all of us because Adam and Eve represent every man and woman - us.

The Bible says that human beings are made in the 'image and likeness' of God. So when we look at others and ourselves we should be able to see something of God.

> Being in the image of God, the human individual possesses the dignity of a *person*, who is not just something, but someone. (CCC 357)

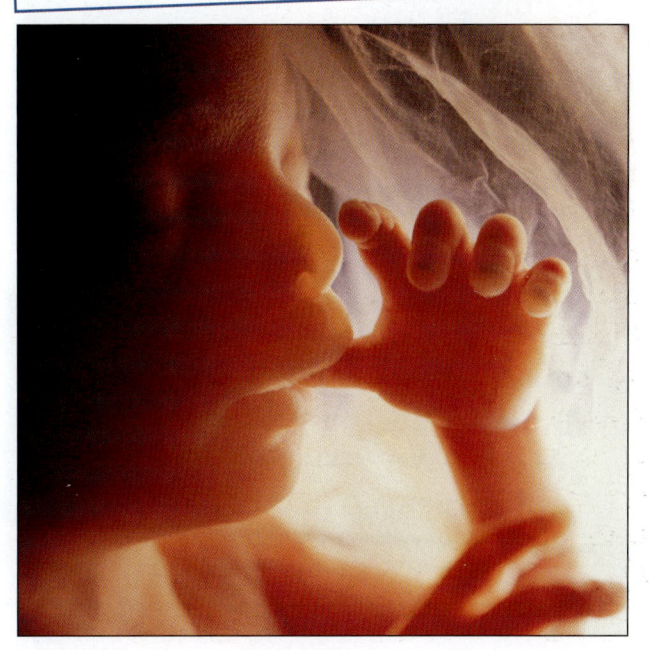

"Before I formed you in the womb I knew you."
(Jeremiah 1:5)

Creation

We are also very special to God: individual and unique. We are not only his creations, but also his children. Look up these three passages from the Bible:

Psalm 139:1, 2, 13-16

This was written nearly three thousand years ago and is in praise of God, his power, and his love for people, for each and every individual. The writer thanks God for looking after him from the moment of conception, even before he was born.

Matthew 6:25-34

In this passage, Jesus tells his followers not to worry too much about material or physical things, but to concentrate on the important things in life, on the 'kingdom'. If we do, God promises us that he will provide everything we need, and that we will be looked after. We must trust him.

Matthew 10:29-31

Here, Jesus assures us that there is no need for us to be afraid. We are precious in God's eyes.

Activities

1. Which of these three readings do you prefer? Give reasons for your choice.

2. Start writing your own autobiography.

(a) Go back to your early memories of childhood. Think of all the good things God has given to you (parents, friends, relatives, your gifts and talents, etc).

My Journey to the Truth
The Early Years

(b) Think of times when life was difficult but you believe God answered your prayers for help.

Describe these experiences.

Glossary
THE TEMPTER, CONCEPTION, MATERIAL THINGS.

Creation

Made in God's Own Image

Read this poem:

I am made in God's own image
because I am alive
and I am clothed in a strength like God's.

I am a person...
free to use the powers
God has given to me:
  the courage to love
  the power to think
  the freedom to choose
  the ability to decide for myself
  the right to make good use
  of all that God has created -
  the mastery of the world itself.

I am a person...
  special and unique
  the only one like me
  who can reflect God in my being.

I am a person...
  a sign of God to others
  because I am made in God's image
  because I have God's light in my heart
  I can mirror God to others.

I show God to others when I am really me,
When I reflect God in my own way.
  This is what it means to be a person.
  This is what it means to be me.
  How often do I think of thanking God
  for making me to be me?

(Adapted from an anonymous source)

Activities

1. Write down all the things about you that are special and unique.

2. Take a few minutes to reflect on the diagram and use it to make a list of what you think are:

  (a) our privileges;
  (b) our responsibilities.

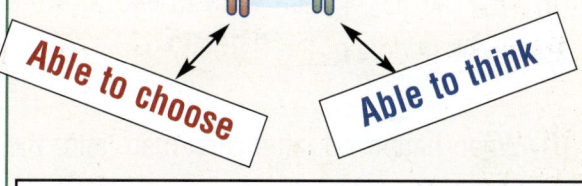

Diagram labels:
- Able to know and love God
- Able to be stewards of Creation
- Able to be creative
- Able to be in a relationship with God
- Having free will
- Able to choose
- Able to think

Human beings made in the image of God

3. How can we 'reflect God' when we meet people who feel:

  (a) scared;
  (b) not as 'good' as us;
  (c) unloved?

Or...

4. In groups, work out a role-play about someone who feels scared, not as 'good' as you, or unloved.

Show how you could make them feel better, how you could 'reflect God' to them.

15

Creation

God's Great Love

In the Bible, we read that Creation was made perfect; it was wonderful; it was beautiful. But then something went wrong. Human beings - Adam and Eve - tried to be God. They refused to obey God. Instead of doing what God wanted them to do, and instead of trusting in his goodness, they deliberately went against his wishes. They wanted their way instead of God's way. As a result they lost God's friendship. This was the 'original' sin; from it, all other sins follow. Read the story for yourself. You will find it in Genesis 2:18-3:24.

Activities

1. Read **Genesis 2:18-3:24**.

(a) What did God tell man?

(b) Describe the Garden.

(c) Why did God make man a companion?

(d) How did God make woman?

(e) Why did the woman want to eat from the tree in the middle of the Garden?

(f) What happened after the man and the woman had eaten the fruit?

(g) What did God say to them?

2. In the story, there are many symbols to help explain Theological Truths. For example, Adam can be seen as a symbol for all humankind. Can you think of the symbolic meanings of the following:

(a) The Garden.

(b) The Serpent.

(c) Eve.

(d) The Tree.

3. In the story of Adam and Eve, we read about their temptation. Can you think of a time when you were tempted? Did you give in to the temptation? What happened? If you were in the same position now, what would you choose to do?

4. (a) What do you think this diagram illustrates?

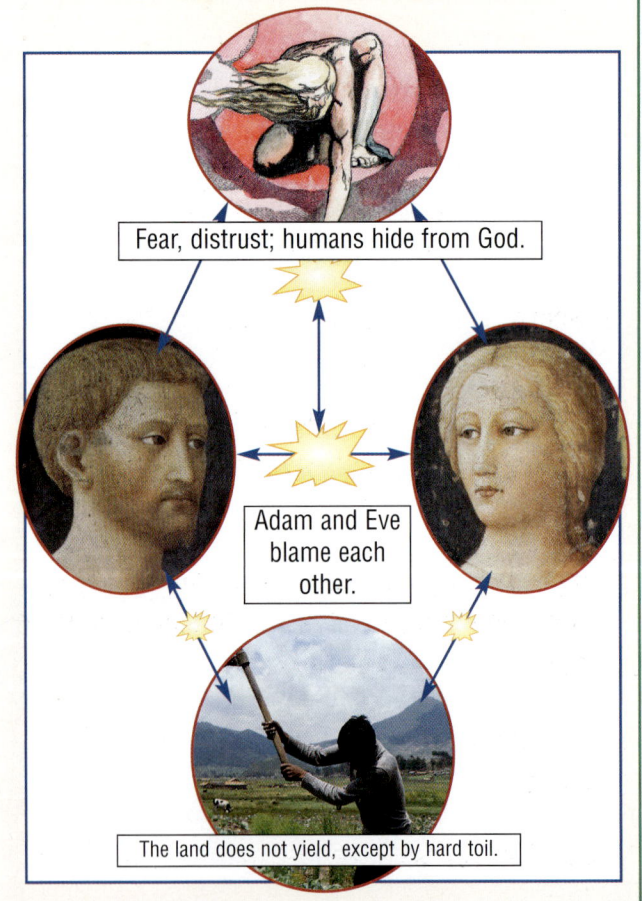

Fear, distrust; humans hide from God.

Adam and Eve blame each other.

The land does not yield, except by hard toil.

(b) What do the explosions represent?

(c) What do you think the lines between the circles represent?

Creation

Activities

A Moment to Reflect

Since God is Creator, and we are made in God's image and likeness, we must be creators too! What have you created today? It may be laughter... or sadness. Have you created a pleasant atmosphere at home or in the classroom? Or maybe an unhappy one. In practical ways, you might have 'created' toast from a slice of bread, or a story or picture from your imagination.

Have you created something from your imagination today?

5. Spend two minutes thinking about today.

(a) List all the things you have 'created' today. When God created the universe, he looked at everything he had made and saw that it was good.

(b) Next to your list, write down GOOD, if it was something positive you created, or BAD next to the negative things.

(c) Are there more 'good' or 'bad' things listed?

(d) Set yourself targets for tomorrow! List them.

6. There are lots of ways in which people are NOT like God. For instance:

when they tell a lie - God is always truthful;

when they are hateful - God is love.

(a) List six other ways in which we behave that are not God-like.

(b) Now take these six ways in which we are not God-like and make some resolutions to show how you will be more God-like in the future. Give examples of each of the resolutions.

Example: Lying

Resolution: When asked whether I have done my homework, I won't make excuses if I haven't, but I will answer honestly, even if it means that I will get into trouble.

Key points to remember

"The transmission of original sin is a mystery that we cannot fully understand. But we do know by Revelation that Adam had received original holiness and justice not for himself alone, but for all human nature. By yielding (giving in) to the tempter, Adam and Eve committed a personal sin, but this sin affected the human nature that they would then transmit (pass on) in a fallen state." (CCC 404)

Glossary

REVELATION, FALLEN STATE.

Creation

Stewards of the Earth

When God created people, the Bible tells us that he said:

> "Let them have dominion over the fish in the sea, and over the birds of the air, and over the cattle, and over all the wild animals of the earth, and over every creeping thing that creeps upon the earth." *(Genesis 1:26)*

In accepting our part in Creation, we need to be in harmony with God's purposes. When God saw what he had created, he knew that it was good. Since we are made in God's 'image and likeness', we are able to know and appreciate goodness - to be able to look at Creation as God did and say 'It is good'! But we are also responsible for developing the good in Creation, in ourselves, in others and in the world at large.

Humankind is part of the world. The way we act can either help nature or harm it.

Ultimately, we have the power to destroy it, or to preserve it, to look after it or to harm it. This is what is meant by 'dominion'. We are called to be stewards or caretakers of God's Creation.

A beautiful ocean with a victim of an oil slick.

Activities

1. Make a list (or a poster) of some of the beautiful things in our world. You could use a collage of newspaper/ magazine cuttings.

2. Describe the most beautiful place you have ever seen. You must say why you think it is beautiful. Look at this example.

> "There is a lovely road that runs from Ixopo into the hills. These hills are grass-covered and rolling and they are lovely beyond any singing of it. The road climbs seven miles into them, to Carisbrooke; and from there, if there is no mist, you look down on one of the fairest valleys in Africa..."
> *(Cry, the Beloved Country, by Alan Paton)*

3. You have learnt that God wants everyone to be a good steward of his world. A good steward is someone who looks after things well.

Make a checklist of things you could do to be a good steward where you are. Set out your work like the example below. There is an 'ideas bank' to help you.

I could be a good steward in my school by...
I could be a good steward in my home by...
I could be a good steward in my neighbourhood by...

eating healthy food   not wasting food
using only as much water as I need to use
taking care of my health
trying to be tidy
re-using carrier bags
helping to clean up, even when I've not made a mess
showing care to others
switching off lights that are not needed
treating animals with care
recycling glass, cans and paper

Glossary
DOMINION.

Creation

Is it too late?

As Christians, we believe that we are entrusted with the earth - that we are stewards or caretakers of God's Creation. But we also believe that God continues to care for our world and us. Some scientists, politicians, business-people and others are recognising that we are in danger of damaging and even destroying the planet, or at least vast areas of it. Wildlife - animals, birds, fish, plants and insects - are under threat. The air we breathe is polluted, the ice caps at the poles are melting, and water levels are rising, threatening considerable areas of land. But it is not too late if we all act now.

Steps have already been taken. The lawmakers now place stricter controls on what chemicals are released into the air; in our daily lives, we are encouraged to recycle bottles, cans and paper. If we are to save our planet, some major decisions will have to be made and acted upon. Such decisions will almost certainly influence the way we live now. For instance, we may have to restrict the amount we drive, or the way we dispose of waste.

"Live simply, so that others may simply live!"

Scientists and economists tell us that there are enough natural resources, including food, to enable everyone to have enough to eat and to have access to the things they need to have a decent quality of life. Some people claim there are too many people for the earth to sustain, that our planet is over-populated, and the situation is getting worse. But if we, as stewards of Creation, were to re-distribute food and resources fairly - giving less to those who have more than they need, and more to those who do not have enough - we would find that there is enough for everyone.

Ways in which we can improve our stewardship of the environment.

Activities

1. What can we do to stop humans destroying so much of the natural world? Draw up an action plan, suggesting at least four things - one of which should be to do with the way we ourselves live our everyday lives.

2. Plan an Assembly. You must include:

(a) a brief description of an environmental issue, e.g. endangered species, pollution, global warming;

(b) an explanation of why this issue is an abuse of God's Creation;

(c) a statement of Christian teaching on stewardship;

(d) suggestions for action that you can take in order to be responsible stewards in the school and neighbourhood.

(e) Write a prayer or choose a hymn to conclude the Assembly.

Research

3. Look at the CAFOD website: www.cafod.org.uk.

Find out how CAFOD is helping to redistribute the wealth of the world.

Glossary
STEWARDSHIP.

Creation

The End of Paradise... But Still a Promise

We have seen from the story of Creation in Genesis that Adam and Eve - who represent all people - rejected the paradise God intended for them. When faced with the choice of good or evil, right or wrong, they were selfish and in effect said to God: 'We don't want it - have it back!'

They had chosen to reject God and all the wonderful things he offered; the consequence was sin, suffering and death. But remember that temptation comes along for all of us, every minute of the day.

God's Love

God showed the extent of his love for us by sending his own son, Jesus, to bring us back to him. Jesus is the Way, the Truth and the Life for us.

"I am the Way, the Truth and the Life. No one can come to the Father except through me." (John 14:6)

Activities

1. Imagine you have given a wonderful present to a friend and they reject it.

   (a) Close your eyes for a few minutes and think about it.

   (b) Write down how you feel.

2. Adam and Eve have to tell their children the story of what happened to them. They have to explain how they made a mess of things not only for themselves, but also for everybody else.

   Imagine you are either Adam or Eve. Write an account of what happened and express your sorrow for falling into temptation.

3. What is the message in all of this for us today?

Key points to remember

In the beginning, God created everything. The Creation is the first revelation of God's love. God and his creatures, including humankind, live in perfect harmony and joy.

With access to the 'Tree of Life', God offers humanity the gift of eternal life.

By choosing evil rather than good, people choose to reject God's gift. The consequence is suffering and death.

In the person of Jesus, life is restored and death is overcome. Jesus is the second great revelation of God's boundless love. In union with him, we are charged with showing God's love to the world by loving each other.

God loved the world so much that he gave his only Son, so that everyone who believes may not perish but may have eternal life. (John 3:16)

This is the ideal towards which all Christians strive: to bring the kingdom of God into being on earth. To be instruments in forming a world of love and happiness, peace and harmony, where there will be no more death or sin, no more mourning or pain. To be partners with God in creating 'a new heaven and a new earth' - a 'new creation'.

2 Covenant
Promises

I Promise!

All of us make promises every day...

"I want you to promise to do your homework."

"I promise to pay back that £5 you lent me."

"If I let you use my calculator, will you promise to give it back to me after class?"

"I promise I'll be good."

Some of them have conditions attached: If I promise to do something for you, you have to promise to do something for me...

"If you lend me your pen, I promise I'll let you listen to my new CD."

"If you promise to tidy your room, I'll promise to play a computer game with you later."

Other promises are really important and should never be taken lightly. For example, when someone starts a job, they promise to work hard, and the employer agrees to pay him or her a wage and allow them time off for holidays. Or, when someone dies, they usually leave a Will promising that the people they loved can have some of the things that they have left behind.

Covenant Promise

A solemn promise between two people or groups of people is called a 'Covenant'. The covenant is made when the people accept it and they undertake to fulfil their part of it. For example, when a man and a woman get married, they solemnly promise to love each other completely for the rest of their lives. For his part, God promises to be faithful to the married couple and give them the help they need. This is his Covenant with them.

A wedding ceremony is a sign of a promise between a man and a woman who love each other.

Covenant

Activities

1. Use the phrases in the boxes below to write out two examples of promises: one that is easy to keep, and one that is very hard. Boxes can be used more than once. Use the first box to start off both examples.

I'll keep my side of the promise	if you keep yours	and if you let me down or hurt me	I'll take back my promise.
	even if you don't keep yours	and even if you let me down or hurt me	I might forgive you, but only once.
			I'll keep trying to forgive you and keep my promise.

2. Think of a promise you have made recently. You do not have to say what the promise was, but you may do so if you wish.

(a) To whom was the promise made?

(b) Were there any conditions attached? (If I promise to do this, you must promise to do that.)

(c) Why did you make the promise?

(d) Did you keep this promise? Why/ why not?

(e) What happened as a result?

(f) What have you learnt about yourself from this?

3. Pick one of the following statements.

Explain whether you agree with the statement or not.

(a) You do not have to keep a promise someone forced you to make.

(b) The greatest promises involve the most risk.

(c) A promise made in writing must be kept; a promise made in words need not be.

(d) The best way to get through life is to avoid making any promises to anyone.

Key points to remember

When God makes a promise, we know that it will always be kept. That promise is as true today as it was thousands of years ago.

"Although man can forget God or reject him, He never ceases to call every man to seek him, so as to find life and happiness." (CCC 30)

"Even when he disobeyed you and lost your friendship you did not abandon him to the power of death …Again and again you offered a covenant to man…" (Eucharistic Prayer IV)

The First Covenant

God made a covenant with the Israelites. In fact, God made several covenants with them, but the main one was that they would always be looked after and protected. In the covenant, God chooses to invite people into a loving relationship with him.

The Bible is a book of stories about people. The Israelites tried to make sense of the world around them. There were lots of things they did not understand, just as today we are still searching for answers to some questions.

The Israelites believed in God. They believed God was good and was responsible for the whole of creation, but they also experienced suffering and pain.

The story of Noah is about a great flood that covered the earth because the people had become corrupt. Only Noah was found to be just and upright - and so he survived with his family. They sailed across the flood in a large boat or ark, with two animals of every kind on board. The person who wrote this story was trying to answer some big questions and explain some mysteries.

Once the rain had stopped and they were on dry land again, Noah thanked God for saving him and his family. In this story God showed how special the whole human family is by making a covenant - a solemn promise - with Noah: that the world would never be destroyed by flooding again.

In the story of Noah, the rainbow is a symbol. The Israelites would look at it and remember the promise that God made to them: that they were God's special people and that the world would never be destroyed again by flooding.

The rainbow is the sign of God's first covenant with Noah.

That promise is still true today; God is always faithful to a promise.

Activities

1. Put the boxes below in order and write a paragraph to sum up the meaning of the Noah story. [Clue: words beginning with... complete a sentence.]

- God rescued those who loved him from...
- Their faithfulness brought down a blessing for all in that...
- ...this destructive chaos swamping everything.
- People's wrongdoing led to...
- ...God would never allow chaos to destroy the order he'd put into Creation.
- ...self-destruction and chaos.
- ...God gave his faithful few a new future in a renewed world.

2. Look at the picture of the rainbow. What are the seven colours in it? Suggest something that each of these colours represent. Here is one to start you off: GREEN for the earth. Now over to you.

Glossary
COVENANT, SYMBOL.

Covenant

God's Covenant with Abraham

The Bible is full of stories about God doing amazing things.

People say: It can't be done!

God says: Oh yes it can! And then he does it.

Abraham, who was first called Abram, was a man of great faith. His faith in God was so strong that he was ready to give up everything to do God's will.

One day he heard God saying to him:

The Negeb Desert, through which Abram and his family travelled.

"Leave your country, your family and your father's house, for the land I will show you. I will make you a great nation; I will bless you and make your name so famous that it will be used as a blessing." (Gen. 12:1-2)

Abram did not want to go. He was already old, already rich and already settled. He tried to shut out the voice, but it kept coming back. Try to imagine what it must have been like for him to leave his house and friends and set out for an unknown land.

However, being a man of faith, he took his wife, Sarai, his nephew, Lot, and all the possessions they could carry and set off. He was not quite sure which route to take so he trusted all the time that God would guide him. On his journey he passed through mountains and desert. The desert was a very hot, dry place - a vast unknown territory. People easily got lost and died there. Many months passed, Abram still trusted in God, he believed he was doing what God wanted him to do.

From the Negeb desert Abram went down into Egypt. Again the voice of the Lord God spoke to him in a vision:

"Have no fear, Abram, I am your shield: your reward will be great." (Gen. 15:1)

Years later when Abram had become a very old man, an extraordinary event took place. God appeared to him and said:

"I will make a Covenant between myself and you, and increase your numbers greatly." (Gen. 17:2)

Abram was astonished and bowed to the ground and God said this to him:

"Here now is my covenant with you: you shall become the father of a multitude of nations. You shall no longer be called Abram; your name shall be Abraham, for I make you father of a multitude of nations... I will establish my Covenant between myself and you, and your descendants after you, generation after generation... and I will be your God." (Gen. 17:6-8)

Covenant

Abraham was now truly bewildered: how could this possibly come about? He was very old and his wife was much too old to have a family; but again God spoke to Abraham:

"As for Sarai your wife, you shall not call her Sarai, but Sarah. I will bless her and moreover give you a son by her." (Gen. 17:15)

This seems an incredible story, but all that God said came true and Sarah gave birth to a son whom she called Isaac.

Activities

1. Imagine you are Sarah. Re-tell the story from her point of view and include the questions she must have been asking Abraham.

Use the following texts from Genesis to guide you:

12:1-9	the call of Abraham, God's promise of the land and the journey;
17:1-8	the Covenant and Abraham's response;
17:15-19	the promise of a baby, the start of the new nation;
21:1-7	the birth of Isaac.

Key points to remember

The story of Abraham is a story of faith. God made several promises to him: that he would have a land to live in, he would have a son, and a great nation would be descended from him. God made a Covenant with Abraham, and all that he promised came true. Down through the ages Abraham has become known as 'our father in faith'.

We are the descendants of Abraham and we have inherited God's great blessings. In return God wants us to recognise and love him as our God, to trust him, and to have faith in him. This is what he asks of us today.

Abraham, our father in faith.

Glossary
NEGEB DESERT, MULTITUDE OF NATIONS.

25

Covenant

The Story of the Exodus and the Passover

Abraham and Isaac's descendants (the Israelites) settled in Egypt during a time of famine. At first they were well treated, but as many years passed they became slaves of the Egyptians and were forced to do very hard work. They had to make bricks and help to build the cities of Pithom and Rameses in the Nile delta.

They were scared and depressed. But they remembered that God had promised he would always look after them and protect them. He had made a covenant with them, and God always keeps his word. So when the people prayed to God, in their misery and slavery, he answered their prayers. (Exodus 2:23-25)

God calls Moses

God decided that the best way to help his people was to get them out of Egypt and to a land of their own. There were two problems though. Firstly, the Egyptians did not want to let them go. The Israelites helped the Egyptians to live comfortably, because they did all the hard work, especially building the cities. The second problem was: Who would lead the Israelites out of Egypt? The person God chose was called Moses.

Charlton Heston as Moses in the film 'The Ten Commandments'.

26

Covenant

Who was Moses?

God chose Moses to lead his people out of Egypt and to bring them into the wilderness so that he could make a covenant with them. Our task is to research the character of Moses, and we find information about him in the first few chapters of the Book of Exodus.

Chapter 2

- *The birth of Moses*
- *His escape at birth and his Egyptian upbringing*
- *His later escape to Midian*
- *His marriage to Zipporah*

Chapter 3

- *God calls Moses in the Burning Bush*
- *Moses' reaction to God's call*

Chapter 4

- *God gives Moses miraculous power*
- *Moses tells God that he is not a good public speaker so God offers him a solution*
- *Moses returns to Egypt*

Chapter 5

- *Moses and his brother, Aaron, go to Pharaoh*

Chapter 6

- *God renews the covenant*

Chapter 7, 8, 9, 10

- *The first nine plagues*

Covenant

Activities

Work in groups

Each group takes a section of the Book of Exodus: make sure that all the chapters listed on page 27 are covered.

1. Read the text. Make a summary of the main points about Moses. These should be in a list, so that they can be added to those of the other groups to make a Fact File on Moses.

2. Using the information you have collected, discuss these questions.

(a) What have you learnt about Moses' character?

(b) What have you learnt about how God deals with the people he chooses?

(c) Do you think Moses was a good choice? Give reasons for your answer.

(d) What still puzzles you?

3. As a class, collect together all your information about Moses. Discuss your answers to Question 2.

4. Design a poster or a newspaper advertisement for someone to lead the Israelites out of slavery in Egypt.

You might want to look in the jobs section of your local or regional newspaper for design hints and for the kind of questions to be asked.

Situation Vacant

Explain:

- What sort of person you will need.

- What he (or she) will have to do to carry out the job.

- What the risks and benefits of this job might be.

- What sort of qualities might be needed.

---

5. Look at your poster or advert, and decide whether you would like the job or not. Explain your decision.

6. Read Exodus 3:7-10.

Now look again at your advert or poster with the details of the sort of person you would have chosen.

(a) What would be the difference between the person you have chosen, and Moses?

(b) What would be the same?

Glossary
NILE DELTA, WILDERNESS, MIRACULOUS.

Covenant

God Speaks to Moses

The Plagues

"I have seen the miserable state of my people... I send you to Pharaoh to bring the sons of Israel, my people, out of Egypt."

However, Moses felt he would not be able to undertake such a difficult task and said to God: *"Who am I to go to Pharaoh and bring the sons of Israel out of Egypt?" (Exodus 3:7-11)*

"What if they will not believe me or listen to my words...?" *(Exodus 4:1)*

"But, my Lord, never in my life have I been a man of eloquence, either before or since you have spoken to your servant. I am a slow speaker and not able to speak well." (Exodus 4:10-11)

In the burning bush, God described himself simply as I AM. In other words, God IS. He never changes. He can always be depended upon and trusted. He is always with us. And that was the message that Moses had to take back to the Israelites. That he had heard their prayers and was going to lead them out of Egypt and away from their miserable lives of slavery. But when Moses and his brother Aaron went to see Pharaoh - the king of the Egyptians - they were not welcomed at all.

God, through Moses, commanded Pharaoh nine times: *"Let my people go"*. Each time Pharaoh refused, God sent a plague that caused widespread destruction throughout Egypt.

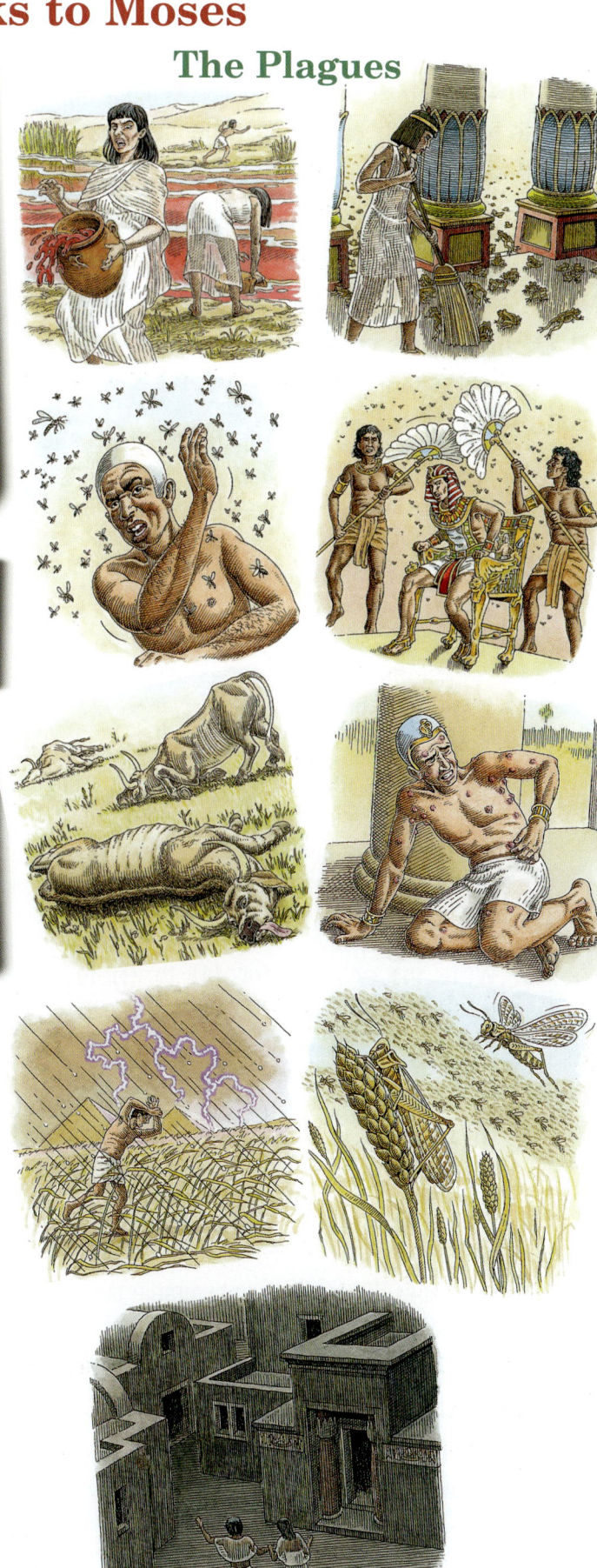

29

Covenant

Activities

1. Moses had difficulty believing he was the right man for the job God was asking him to do. He lacked confidence and he was not a good speaker.

   (a) Describe two ways in which God helped him. Support your answer with reference to: Exodus 4:1-17.

   (b) What is the message in this story for each one of us?

2. Read Exodus 5:1-9. What immediate effect did the visit of Moses and Aaron to Pharaoh have on the lives of the Israelites?

Consider the following in your answer:

   (a) What reason did Moses and Aaron give Pharaoh for letting the Israelites go?

   (b) Why did Pharaoh refuse?

   (c) What was the punishment Pharaoh gave the Israelites after Moses and Aaron had been to see him?

   (d) Whom did the Israelites blame?

3. Write the answers for **(a)** to **(j)** in one sentence each.

(a) What does the word Exodus mean?
   (i) mass departure;
   (ii) freedom;
   (iii) slavery.

(b) Why did the King of Egypt decide to oppress the Israelites?
   (i) because they would not worship false gods;
   (ii) because they were great in number;
   (iii) because they were cruel to Egyptians.

(c) Why did Moses flee to Midian? Because:
   (i) the Pharaoh discovered that he was an Israelite;
   (ii) the Pharaoh's son was jealous of him;
   (iii) he killed an Egyptian and the story got out.

(d) Where was Moses when God called him?
   (i) Canaan;
   (ii) Mount Sinai;
   (iii) Egypt.

(e) How did God appear to Moses?
   (i) in the shape of a burning bush;
   (ii) in a brilliant light;
   (iii) as a dove.

(f) Why was Moses instructed to remove his shoes? Because:
   (i) they would be burnt up;
   (ii) he was to wash his feet in a nearby stream;
   (iii) he was standing on holy ground.

(g) What answer was given to Moses after he asked for the name of God?
   (i) I Am who I Am;
   (ii) Israel;
   (iii) Abraham.

(h) How was the promised land described?
   (i) a land of milk and honey;
   (ii) a land of palms and springs;
   (iii) a land of great forests, mountains and valleys.

(i) What is the first sentence of Exodus 6:7?
   (i) 'I am the God of Abraham, of Isaac and of Jacob.'
   (ii) 'I have heard the groaning of the sons of Israel.'
   (iii) 'I will adopt you as my own people, and I will be your God.'

(j) What was the worst plague visited on Egypt?
   (i) the plague of the river of blood;
   (ii) the death of all the first-born, human and animal;
   (iii) the plague of darkness.

Glossary

SONS OF ISRAEL, EXODUS, FIRST-BORN.

The Passover

Nine times Moses tried to convince Pharaoh, the Egyptian king, to let the Israelites go free, but every time he refused. Eventually, Pharaoh was given one last chance. Unless the Israelites were allowed to leave, Moses told him, God would send one final plague: the death of all the first born human and animal. The eldest sons of all the Egyptians - including Pharaoh's own - would die.

The Israelites were given instructions to make sure that it was obvious which houses belonged to them: no harm would come to people inside. They were also told to get ready for the journey. These were the preparations they had to make.

Preparation...

They had to cook and eat a special meal. It was to be roast lamb, served with bitter herbs (vegetables) and with bread made without yeast, because they would not have time to wait for the bread to rise. This was known as unleavened bread. Any bit of the roast lamb that was not eaten had to be burnt.

Waiting...

They had to be ready for a quick getaway after the meal.

With cloaks and sandals on, they had to eat standing up, so that they would be able to leave immediately, as soon as Pharaoh gave the word.

Protection...

They were to mark the doorframes of their houses with blood from the lamb prepared for the meal.

That would be a clear sign that these were the homes of Israelites, not Egyptians.

Covenant

Passover...

The Lord was true to his word. That night - after the eldest sons of the Egyptians had died - Pharaoh agreed to let the Israelites go. Their own sons had been spared: the angel of death had passed over their houses. That is why they called this event the Passover, and why Jewish families still celebrate the Passover to this very day.

Exodus...

The Israelites set out on their journey. This is known as the Exodus, which means leaving or setting out. The book in the Bible that contains this story is also called Exodus because it is the account of the Israelites' journey from Egypt to the land God gave them.

The story of the Exodus is about the weak and the powerless eventually winning - being victorious - because they put their faith in God. True to his word, God guided and protected the Israelites as they left Egypt. But once they reached the banks of the Red Sea, they panicked. How were they going to get across?

Meanwhile, back in Egypt...

Pharaoh was having second thoughts. He led his army out to bring the Israelites back. With the Red Sea in front of them, and Pharaoh's soldiers approaching from behind, the odds against them seemed impossible. Slaughter seemed inevitable.

The Covenant...

Moses trusted in God. If God had promised to save and protect his people, God would not let them down. God had made a covenant, so God would be true to his word.

And sure enough, once again, the impossible became possible. Moses lifted his staff and the Red Sea opened and let the people of Israel through.

Covenant

Activities

> Israel witnessed the great act that the Lord had performed against the Egyptians, and the people venerated the Lord; they put their faith in the Lord and Moses, his servant.
> *(See Exodus 14:21-31)*

1. Read Exodus 14:21-31.

2. Imagine you are one of the Israelite children. Your family is preparing for the Passover meal. There is anticipation that you might at last be getting away from Egypt and slavery. Write a letter to a friend telling them about the preparations. Remember the following points.

(a) Who is there with you in your home?

(b) How are your parents preparing the meal?

(c) What sort of atmosphere is there in your house? How do people feel - including you?

(d) How are you all preparing for the journey?

(e) What happens to the blood from the lamb? Finish your letter with the line:
I'll write again when we get away from Egypt.

3. Complete the following sentences. Deuteronomy 26:8 will help you.

(a) It was ☐ who led the Israelites out of Egypt.

(b) With ☐ hand, and ☐ arm.

(c) With ☐ ☐, and with signs and ☐.

Key points to remember

God's Promise

The escape from Egypt was only part of the story. God had also promised the Israelites a land of their own. They were on their way now. This is another reason why their descendants today still celebrate the Passover. It recalls not only their escape from slavery, but also their beginnings as a nation with their own land.

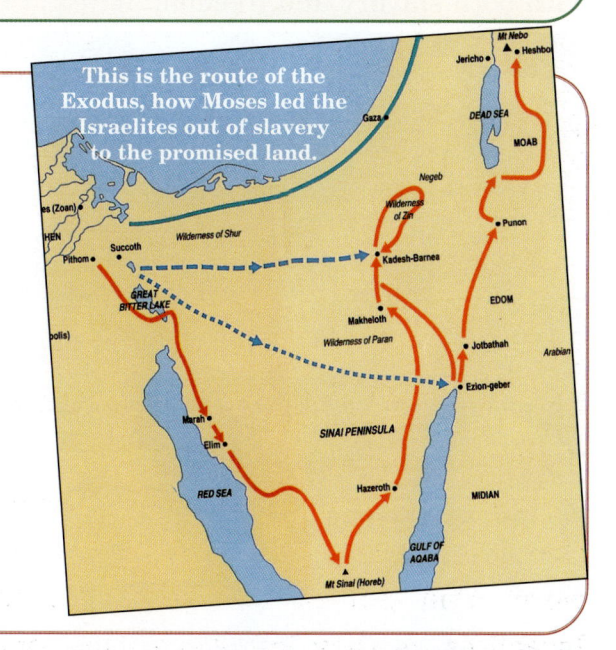

This is the route of the Exodus, how Moses led the Israelites out of slavery to the promised land.

Glossary
PASSOVER, ANCESTORS, YEAST, UNLEAVENED BREAD, RED SEA.

Covenant

The Passover Today

For over 3,000 years, Jews (the descendants of the Israelites) have continued to celebrate the Passover. For them, it not only recalls their escape from Egypt and slavery, but also the start of their own nation. Most importantly, it is a celebration of God's goodness and faithfulness to the Covenant.

God commanded the Israelites to mark their freedom with an annual festival called Pesach. The Pesach commemorates their total reliance on God's help, for no human power could have taken them out of slavery. The celebration takes the form of a special meal called the Seder. The meal follows a special order that is set down in a book known as the Hagadah (telling of the story).

The story is not only told through words. Each item of food on the Seder plate is a symbol calling to mind a different aspect of the story. Because the Jews are celebrating the passage from slavery to freedom most of the symbolic foods have associations with both slavery and freedom.

The Seder Dish.

Word Bank

Chametz
bread that contains yeast or grain

Matzah
unleavened bread

Hagadah
telling the story

Seder
Passover meal

Haroset
apple and honey

Why is this night different?

At every Seder (Passover Meal), the youngest member of the family asks the head of the household four questions.

- On all other nights we may eat chametz or matzah. Tonight, why do we eat only matzah?

- On all other nights we may eat any kind of herbs. Tonight, why do we eat bitter herbs?

- On all other nights we do not dip our food at all. Tonight, why do we dip twice?

- On all other nights we eat sitting or leaning. Tonight, why do we all lean?

Covenant

*"Blessed art thou, O Lord, our God,
King of the universe,
who hast sanctified us with thy
commandments, and commanded
us to eat unleavened cakes".*

Taking some of the bitter herbs he says:

*"Blessed art thou, O Lord, our God,
King of the universe,
who hast sanctified us with
thy commandments,
and commanded us to eat
bitter herbs".*

During the Seder these questions are answered as the family read through the Hagadah. For example, the head of the household takes half of the middle matzah out of the dish and says:

Activities

1. Copy these sentences into your exercise book, adding the missing words:

(a) _____ is the ingredient in bread that makes it rise. Bread made without this ingredient is called _____ .

(b) Haroset is made from nuts, honey and _____ . It represents the bricks that the Israelites used to make to build the _____ when they were slaves in Egypt.

(c) _____ from the lamb was splashed on the doorposts of the Israelites' houses so that the angel of death would pass over. Today, Jews use a _____ instead of a whole lamb at the Passover meal.

2. Read Exodus 13:8, 14 & 15, and then complete these sentences, copying them into your exercise book.
(a) This night is different from all other nights because...
(b) We celebrate the Passover tonight because...

3. Design a fact sheet for pupils younger than yourself, explaining the Passover Meal. You will have to do some research to find out the significance of some of the items listed on the Seder plate. Explain what each of the ingredients represents. Illustrate your fact-sheet. Help the pupils to understand why the meal is so important to Jews today.

Try: www.passover.net for help.

4. There are probably lots of other questions you would like to ask the head of the household about the Passover. Write down at least three, then try and find out the answers for yourself.

Try: www.kosher4passover.com for help.

Research

5. Explain why during the Seder:
(a) they drink four cups of wine; (Clue: Exodus 6:6-7; four reasons are given).
(a) some of the food is dipped in salt water;
(a) Matzah is eaten.

Glossary
PESACH, SEDER, HAGADAH, CHAMETZ, MATZAH, BITTER HERBS.

Covenant

The Ten Commandments

A Code for Living

Every time a driver gets behind the wheel of a car, he or she is supposed to follow certain rules. Those rules are contained in a book called 'The Highway Code'.

They answer questions like:

What side of the road should I drive on? How fast should I drive? What should I do if I see a red traffic light in front of me? How do I let other drivers know I intend to turn right?

When drivers follow these rules, driving is easier and safer. They all drive on the same side of the road, at speeds which enable them to stop if there is a hold-up ahead. They stop at junctions - especially ones with traffic lights. They use their indicators to show other drivers that they are intending to turn left or right.

When they disobey these rules, the roads become more dangerous. People drive selfishly, without thinking of other road users, including cyclists and pedestrians. There are accidents. People get hurt or even killed. Imagine what it would be like if everybody just had their own rules!

When the Israelites left Egypt, God gave them a set of rules: their own 'Highway Code' for life. These rules are meant to make life safer and easier. When they are followed, people live together peacefully and happily. They show consideration and respect for each other. Even though there are only ten of them, they cover every aspect of life.

They are known as the Ten Commandments. The Bible tells us that God gave them to Moses on top of Mount Sinai, between Egypt and the land they were heading for.

The Ten Commandments

1. I am the Lord your God. You shall not worship false gods instead of me.

2. You shall not take the name of the Lord your God in vain.

3. Remember to keep holy the Sabbath.

4. Honour your father and your mother.

5. You shall not kill.

6. You shall not commit adultery.

7. You shall not steal.

8. You shall not bear false witness against your neighbour.

9. You shall not covet your neighbour's spouse.

10. You shall not covet your neighbour's goods.

Covenant

These commandments enabled the Israelites to start living together as civilised people. But they are as relevant today as they were 3,000 years ago. They state what is required in the love of God and love of neighbour. The first three are about the love of God, and the other seven about how we should treat the people around us.

The God of the Israelites (the Jews) and the Christians - our God - is a very personal God. He cares for us and knows each one of us individually. The Law, the Ten Commandments, are his instructions for life, designed to enable us to live in harmony with him and with each other.

God has promised us that he will always look after us and protect us: that is his covenant with us. All he asks in return is that we keep his commandments and share his love.

When Jesus was asked which was the greatest commandment, he summarised them in this way:

> "You shall love the Lord your God with all your heart, and with all your soul, and with all your mind... (And) you shall love your neighbour as yourself."
> *(Matthew 22:37-39)*

Activities

1. Read Exodus 19:1-6.
 (a) What is the most important message that God is giving to Moses and the Israelites in this passage?
 (b) Is there a message in it for us to day? Give reasons for your answer.

2. Learn the Ten Commandments.

3. Re-write the Commandments in your own words and give an example of how you might achieve each one in your daily life. For instance, you might re-write the fifth Commandment (you shall not kill):

You should have respect for all life.

Example: being kind to other people; avoiding calling people names or spreading stories; defending a person who is bullied.

4. Imagine that everyone in your hometown decided to keep the commandments for a year.

Describe what difference it would make to the life of:
- police officer;
- a shopkeeper;
- an elderly person;
- and you.

Research

5. Find out what you can about Mount Sinai.

Using reference books, the Internet and/or other resources, write a description of the area in the style of a travel guide or brochure, telling people what it is like and encouraging them to visit.

Glossary
FALSE GODS, SABBATH, HONOUR, ADULTERY, FALSE WITNESS, COVET, SPOUSE, NEIGHBOUR.

Covenant

Key points to remember
Covenant between God and Israel

"I will be your God and you will be my people."

This summarises the covenant between God and Israel.

By saying "I will be your God," God is telling us: "I will be the One to worship, who hears every true prayer, who guides and protects you, who has tender compassion for the needy, and who settles you, Israel, peacefully in the land I gave you..."

By saying "You will be my people," God is telling us: "Remember that I alone am God; do not 'fob me off' with empty rituals but give me your whole self; obey the Law I gave you - for this Law leads to life; show compassion as I have shown compassion... ."

The New Covenant with Jesus

"I will establish a new covenant with the house of Israel... I will put my laws into their minds, and write it on their hearts, I will be their God, and they shall be my people."
(Hebrews 8:8-10, cf. Jeremiah 31:31-34)

In Jesus - especially in his death and resurrection - we enter into a new Covenant with God. We now have the promise of eternal life, of the end of sin and death, of everlasting joy with him.

Our baptismal promises show our willingness to abide by the terms of the covenant between God and ourselves.

Glossary
SAVIOUR, MESSIAH.

3 Exploring the Mass

Going to Mass, joining in the prayer of the Mass, is the most important thing that Catholics do. It is so important that in times of persecution people have given up all they owned, all their belongings and even their very lives, in order to go to Mass. Others risked their lives by giving shelter to the priest who had come to celebrate Mass with them.

In these lessons you will learn about the Mass and all that it contains. This will help you to understand what happens during the Mass and why it is so precious and unique. I realise that you will have been to Mass many times. But it is such a rich mystery that there is always more to learn about it.

Abraham and the Three Angels.

In these lessons you will also have the opportunity to think about what the Mass means to you and how you can take part in it more fully. When people say that they are bored during Mass, I think that is partly due to the fact that they do not know how to join in the Mass in their hearts and in their minds. I hope these lessons will help you to learn how to do so. Step by step you will come to treasure the Mass yourselves.

✠ Archbishop Vincent Nichols

In Exploring the Mass you will:

- **reflect on the reasons for going to Mass;**

- **understand the signs and symbols used at Mass;**

- **know that at Mass we are invited to 'call to mind our sins' and ask for God's forgiveness;**

Exploring the Mass

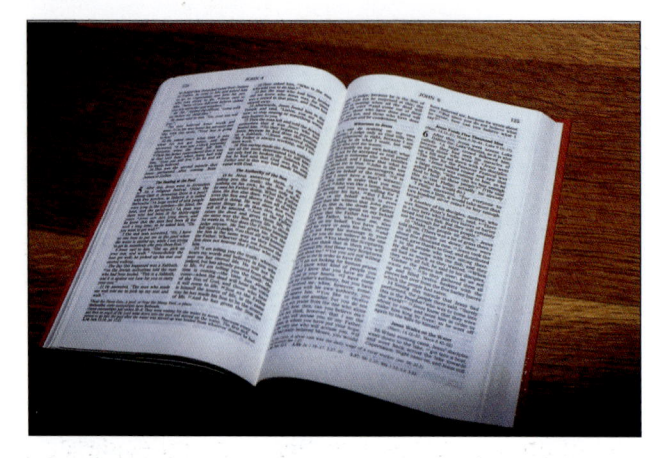

- understand that God speaks to us in the readings at Mass;

- know that we participate in Jesus' Last Supper and sacrifice;

- know that at the Consecration, through the power of the Holy Spirit, the bread and wine become the Body and Blood of Jesus;

- understand that when we receive Holy Communion we know, by faith, that it is Jesus we receive;

- appreciate the continuing presence of Jesus in the Blessed Sacrament.

4 The Paschal Mystery
Travelling with Jesus

We are going on a journey. It will be the most important journey of our lives.

We are following a man who has been more than a friend to us. He has inspired us; he has been our teacher. He has shown us things we never thought possible. For example, he has shown us how God wants us to live, how people can live together happily, how we can find God in each other and in the world, and how God wants us to share eternal happiness with him. That man is Jesus.

Yet for two thousand years people have been asking the question: who is this Jesus? Even Jesus himself asked his friends a similar question:

> Jesus and his disciples left for the villages round Caesarea Philippi. On the way there he put this question to his disciples, "Who do people say I am?"
> *(Mark 8:27-28)*

Activities
Mission Impossible?

In order to explore the mystery of Jesus' passion and death we need to know that he is truly God, and as a man he is truly human. Our evidence for this is in the Bible and the Tradition of the Church.

1. In groups, act as detectives to find evidence for one of the following:

(a) Jesus is truly human;

(b) Jesus is truly God;

(c) Jesus is both God and man.

In your evidence you must be able to quote the scripture passage and give the reference. Here are some clues to start you off:

GROUP A
Luke 2:6, Luke 2:40
Matthew 27:54
Luke 4:3, Mark 8:34-38
Matthew 27:45-47

GROUP B
Luke 2:11-12, Luke 3:22
Luke 4:12, Luke 7:11-17
Luke 8:22-35

GROUP C
John 1:1, John 1:9-12, John 1:14
John 3:13, John 3:16-17, John 4:14,
John 5:26

2. Each group presents the evidence it has found.

3. The Catechism of the Catholic Church teaches:

> "The Son of God does not mean that Jesus is part God and part man, nor does it imply he is the result of a confused mixture of the divine and the human. He became truly man while remaining truly God. Jesus Christ is true God and true man." (CCC 464).

Write this statement in your own words.

The Paschal Mystery

Activities

4. Look at these eight pictures of Jesus.

What messages about Jesus do you think each of the artists who painted these pictures was trying to express?

5. Describe these pictures yourself. Identify how they portray Jesus as:

(a) a human person, a man, or

(b) a divine person, as God, or

(c) both human and divine.

6. Other pupils have been puzzled about Jesus being God. Here are some of there questions:

"Why didn't Jesus charge for the miracles he worked?"

"When the soldiers came to arrest him in the Garden of Gethsemane, why didn't he call on his Father to send 'twelve legions of angels' to save him?"(Matthew 26:53)

"In the desert, why didn't he accept the power and the glory when he was tempted?" (Luke 4:6)

What answers would you give to each one of those questions?

7. One of the important reasons for going on this journey with Jesus is to get to know him really well and to find out who he is.

From the information you have been able to gather, write a statement about Jesus. Make it large enough to be displayed in the classroom. Think of as many ways of describing him as you can.

Extension

8. Read what St. Paul wrote about Jesus' humanity and divinity in Philippians 2:5-11.

Give two examples from the life of Jesus to explain what St. Paul is saying.

Glossary
THE PASSION, TRADITION,
LEGIONS, HUMANITY, DIVINITY.

The Paschal Mystery

Holy Week

The Most Important Week in the Year

Every year, Christians all over the world re-live the events of 2,000 years ago in a very deliberate way. They re-trace the steps of Jesus during the last week of his life on earth, day by day, sometimes hour by hour, for a whole week.

It is known as 'Holy Week' and lasts from Palm Sunday to Easter Sunday.

A Palm Sunday Procession in Jerusalem.

Holy Week might seem disastrous to some people, because Jesus was killed on Good Friday. But because Christians believe he rose again from the dead on Easter Sunday, it becomes marvellous. It is so marvellous in fact, that it opens for us a new sharing in God's life and so we call it a 'mystery' - the 'Paschal Mystery'. The word 'paschal' comes from 'Passover' - the festival when the Jews celebrated their liberation from slavery in Egypt (as we have seen in the chapter on Covenant).

So what we mean when we talk about the 'Paschal Mystery' are events that took place 2,000 years ago, during the Jewish Feast of Passover in Jerusalem. Jesus took part in that Festival.

Day by day, we travel with Jesus; we remember what he said, what happened, and who was involved.

We are grateful for the way he left us his own Body and Blood in Holy Communion.

We feel sorrowful on Good Friday, as we know that it was sin - our own sins - which meant he had to die.

But we also share in the glory of the events of Easter Sunday.

When Jesus rose from the dead, he opened the door to eternal life for us.

As Christians, we believe this and we praise God today because we know that Jesus' death on the cross was not the end. We know that joy follows sorrow and life follows death, just as the empty tomb follows Calvary.

Activities

1. The days of Holy Week have special names.

   (a) Find out what Palm Sunday, Maundy Thursday, Good Friday and Easter Sunday mean.

   (b) Write a sentence on each one explaining what they are, to help a younger pupil understand why they are so special to Christians.

Glossary
CALVARY, HOLY WEEK, MYSTERY, PASCHAL, PASSOVER.

The Paschal Mystery

Palm Sunday

Jesus' friends thought that he was going to be triumphant once they reached Jerusalem. But Jesus himself knew that the only way he could bring us totally to God was to suffer and to die. Even though pain, humiliation and death lay ahead, Jesus was determined. This was God's will and he would fulfil it.

We also have to face troubles in our lives. Sometimes, we have to suffer for things we know are right or have to be done. But we have the example of Jesus to follow, and the knowledge that he is always there to give us strength and help us.

Take a few minutes to think about his words:

> "Come to me, all who labour and are heavy laden, and I will give you rest. Take my yoke upon you, and learn from me. For I am gentle and lowly in heart, and you will find rest for your souls. For my yoke is easy, and my burden is light."
> (Matthew 11:28-30)

Welcome to Jerusalem

We are approaching our destination. Just over the hill lies Jerusalem - the capital city, the centre of power.

Jerusalem was Israel's religious headquarters: the Temple dominated the city and all the senior religious leaders lived there, such as Caiaphas, the High Priest.

It was also where there was a strong presence of the Roman army. The man who governed them, Pontius Pilate, was staying in Jerusalem for the Feast of Passover too, to make sure there was no trouble.

Jerusalem at the Time of Christ (map)

At the end of the journey, Jesus and his friends approached Jerusalem from the Mount of Olives, to the east of the city. By now, people had heard he was getting close and started coming out to welcome him.

On this occasion, Jesus did not slip into Jerusalem unnoticed. For once he acknowledged and encouraged the crowd's cheers.

46

The Paschal Mystery

Activities

1. Read Luke 19:28-40.

2. Copy and complete the table below.

PALM SUNDAY

Gospel reference?	
What happened?	
Who was involved?	
Where did it happen?	

3. Now imagine you are one of the disciples - one of Jesus' friends - who had been sent to collect the colt for him. Write your own story - how you felt on that Sunday.

OR

4. You are a reporter on the 'Jerusalem News' and have been sent to cover the events on that Sunday when Jesus arrived in Jerusalem. Describe the scene and report what some of the people involved said about it.

Extension

5. Using the Internet or other sources of reference, find a picture of Jerusalem as it was during the time of the Roman occupation, 2,000 years ago. The reference 'Second Temple' might help you.

Try: www.holylandhotel.com

6. Identify some key sites within the city: the Temple, the Palace of Pontius Pilate (the Roman Governor), the home of Caiaphas (the High Priest), and the Mount of Olives.

Try: www.cptryon.org/prayer/child/lent/holywk/01.html

Or: www.culham.ac.uk/Lent/index.html

The Mount of Olives in Jerusalem today.

Glossary
HUMILIATION, YOKE, THE TEMPLE, HIGH PRIEST.

47

The Paschal Mystery

Activities

3. Find out what each of these words or phrases means, and write down explanations:

- High Priest
- Sanhedrin
- the Christ
- blasphemy
- prophecy

4. Divide into two teams, and prepare for a discussion on the following:

Team A: Write down as many reasons as you can think of which explain why the authorities considered Jesus guilty or a threat;

Team B: List reasons why he should have been released - why they could have said he was innocent.

Based on the evidence and the accusations, would you have freed him or declared him guilty?

5. Jesus' friend, Peter, was afraid of being caught, but he still wanted to see what happened to Jesus. He followed the group to the High Priest's house, but stayed outside.

(a) Read the account of Peter in the courtyard: Matthew 26:69-75.

(b) Write a short drama for four characters: Peter and the three people who challenged him.

6. Below are six phrases, said by six different people, either in the Garden of Gethsemane, the High Priest's house or the courtyard outside. Write them out as sentences:

PEOPLE	PHRASES	PLACES
JESUS	"Rabbi!"	The Courtyard
PETER	"You too are one of his disciples"	The High Priest's House
CAIAPHAS	"He said he would re-build the Temple in three days"	The Garden of Gethsemane
JUDAS	"Put your sword away"	The High Priest's House
A WITNESS	"I do not know him!"	The Courtyard
HIGH PRIEST'S SERVANT	"Are you the Christ?"	The Garden of Gethsemane

(a) matching who said what and where;

(b) number them in the order they took place according to Matthew 26:47-75.

Extension

7. If none of the main characters slept that night, write an essay about what might have happened during that time, either from the point of view of:

(a) Jesus, imprisoned in Caiaphas' house, or

(b) Peter, full of remorse after his denials, or

(c) Caiaphas, the High Priest who convicted Jesus.

Glossary
HIGH PRIEST, SANHEDRIN, THE CHRIST, BLASPHEMY, PROPHECY, REMORSE, DENIALS.

The Trial Before Pilate

In 63 BC - the Romans occupied Israel. They took control, but still allowed the Jews to worship their God and have a king - even though he had no real power.

So, if there was a person who had committed a crime that the Jewish authorities considered deserved the death penalty, they had to refer it to the Roman Governor.

This is what happened on the Friday morning of Holy Week (Good Friday). Having decided at their own trial the night before, that Jesus was guilty of blasphemy, they took him to Pontius Pilate as soon as daylight broke over Jerusalem.

Who was Pontius Pilate?

Pontius Pilate was in charge of Judea - a territory in the Roman Empire - from 26 to 36 AD.

His title was Procurator or Governor. Some people have described him as a mild-mannered, well-meaning man who reluctantly sent Jesus to his death. But evidence suggests the contrary. Those who knew him described him as corrupt, cruel, and greedy.

Pilate clearly was not convinced that Jesus deserved the death penalty. In fact, he stated at least three times: I find no crime deserving death.

Activities

1. Read Luke 23:1-6.

2. The authorities accused Jesus of four 'crimes'.

What were they?

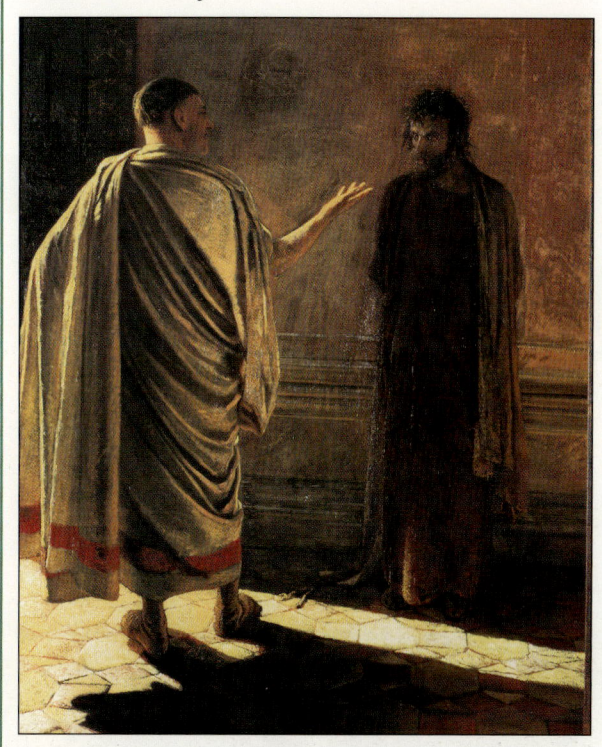

Extension

3. Imagine you are a juror at the trial of Jesus. Think about each of the four accusations.

(a) Can you think of any examples in Jesus' life when he did something that could be considered a crime? Make a list of them.

(b) Write down your reasons for either agreeing with or disagreeing with the accusations.

(c) Write your verdict next to each accusation: Guilty or Not Guilty.

Glossary
ROMAN GOVERNOR, PROCURATOR.

The Paschal Mystery

The Way of the Cross

Every Good Friday in Jerusalem, there is a great procession of people who follow the route Jesus took from Pilate's fortress to Calvary. They even carry a cross through the streets to remind themselves of Jesus' suffering. This route is called the 'Way of Sorrows' or, in Latin, Via Dolorosa.

The 'Way of Sorrows' in Jerusalem.

Although much has changed in Jerusalem over the past 2,000 years, it is still a busy Middle Eastern city.

The buildings you can see there have been constructed over recent centuries, and the souvenirs today are T-shirts and postcards. But the atmosphere through these ancient streets of Jerusalem is still very similar to how it would have been 2,000 years ago.

There are still jostling crowds, merchants trying to sell their goods, people shouting to their friends, children running through the streets, and animals tied at the roadside. Beggars still beg and pilgrims still pray. Jewish devotion is centred on the remains of the Temple.

But for Christians, these streets which join the site of Pontius Pilate's fortress to Calvary (where now there is the Church of the Holy Sepulchre) are very special. By walking along the Via Dolorosa, they are following literally in Jesus' footsteps.

For those of us who cannot be in Jerusalem, we also follow the journey in our churches. Around the walls, you will always see 14 pictures showing 14 stages in the journey. They are known as the Way of the Cross, or Stations of the Cross.

The Paschal Mystery

Activities

1. Read Luke 23: 26-32. Consider the following four people or groups of people:

(a) Mary, Jesus' mother, who had given birth to him in Bethlehem, followed him on his journeys, and now meets her son on the way to his death.

(b) Simon, who was a visitor to Jerusalem from Africa. He probably wondered what all the fuss was about. Then a Roman soldier grabbed him and told him to help this "criminal" who was staggering beneath the weight of his cross.

(c) Veronica was moved to pity when she saw Jesus. He was bruised and bleeding. She took a cloth and wiped his face.

(d) Some of the **women of Jerusalem** were crying at the roadside as Jesus passed, but he told them they should be weeping for themselves and their children because terrible things were going to happen to the city in the future.

Two of them are mentioned in the Gospel accounts of Jesus' journey to his death. Two are not.

(i) Which of them are NOT mentioned in the Gospels?

(ii) Find out what you can about them.

(iii) Why do you think the Church includes them in the Way of the Cross?

2. Put yourself in the position of either Simon from Cyrene, or one of the women of Jerusalem.

(a) Describe what you see as Jesus carries his cross.

(b) Describe what happens;

(c) Describe how you feel.

3. In groups plan an assembly that would help pupils come to a greater understanding of the 'Way of the Cross':

(a) have a reading from scripture;

(b) choose hymns/songs;

(c) compose a prayer or a poem;

(d) could you include a role-play which you have already prepared?

Glossary
CALVARY, VIA DOLOROSA, DEVOTION, HOLY SEPULCHRE (CHURCH OF THE).

The Paschal Mystery

The Death of Jesus

It is virtually impossible for us to imagine the suffering that Jesus experienced on Good Friday.

- His friends had deserted him.
- He had been beaten, whipped and crowned with thorns.
- People spat in his face in front of the crowd.
- He had had a wooden cross forced on him and been made to carry it to Calvary.
- He had been stripped and nailed to that cross.
- And now, he was hanging there, with people all around insulting him, waiting for him to die.

Activities

1. None of us is ever likely to go through as much torment as Jesus. But think of a time when you have been hurt by someone - maybe a bully in school, or a brother or sister. It might have been an accident, rather than deliberate. Or someone might have made fun of you for some reason.

(a) Write about what happened and how you felt.

(b) Did you fight back or leave the confrontation?

(c) Was your reaction to retaliate or to forgive the person who hurt you?

2. Read Luke 23:39-43.

Jesus was not the only one who was crucified on Calvary on Good Friday. Two thieves were also being executed. Jesus said that one of them would be in heaven before the day was over. No matter how hopeless the situation seemed for that man hanging there next to Jesus, he must have been comforted and re-assured by his words.

(a) What does this story tell us about Jesus?

(b) Why do you think Jesus took pity on this criminal?

(c) What message does it have for us today?

(d) If you were to visit somebody in prison, is there a message here that you could bring to the person? What would it be?

The Paschal Mystery

Although he was God, Jesus was also fully human. As he hung on the cross, he felt thirsty. Water might have refreshed him but, instead, a soldier offered him bitter vinegar. After he had taken the vinegar he said:

> *"It is accomplished" and bowing his head he gave up his spirit and died. (John 19:30)*

"It is accomplished!" Those words are so simple and yet so powerful. Jesus is dead but, by dying, he has completed the task that he set out to complete. The journey has reached its end. We have arrived at our destination. But for you - one of his friends who has accompanied him on his travels, who entered Jerusalem with him on Palm Sunday, who felt confident that this week was going to be wonderful - how do you feel?

The Pieta by Michelangelo.

Activities

1. Write your diary entry for Good Friday. Jesus, your friend and master, is dead. Now you are left trying to make sense of it all.

2. What happened after Jesus died? Fill in the missing words. If in doubt, consult John 19. The word bank will help you. You can use a word more than once.

After Jesus died, Joseph of _____ asked _____ for the body of Jesus. Now Joseph was a _____ of Jesus, but secretly because he feared the _____. With _____'s permission, he came and took the body away.

He was accompanied by _____, the man who earlier had visited Jesus at night. _____ brought a mixture of _____ and _____ to embalm the body.

Taking Jesus' body, the two of them _____ it in strips of _____ and treated it with _____. This was in accordance with Jewish burial customs.

At the place where Jesus was crucified, there was a _____, and in it a new _____, in which no one had ever been laid.

Because it was the Jewish day of _____ and since the _____ was nearby, they laid Jesus there.

Word Bank

Jews, spices, Preparation, Myrrh, Nicodemus, Arimathea, garden, Pontius Pilate, wrapped, tomb, Linen, Aloes, Nicodemus, disciple

Glossary
EMBALM, MYRRH, SPICES, ALOES, PIETA.

The Paschal Mystery

Holy Saturday

Watching and waiting

Imagine how Jesus' friends and family felt after they had seen him die and had buried him in the garden tomb.

They could not help but remember - as they gathered together on the Saturday - that Jesus had predicted he would die. He had even told them how he would die! But he had said something else as well: that on the third day he would rise again.

It seemed impossible, but that was what he had said. Death would not be the end. He would live again, and they would see him.

We can look back on the events of Holy Week and Easter, and we know what happened, of course. So, although we might feel sad on Good Friday or Holy Saturday, we also believe that, on Easter Sunday, Jesus did indeed rise from the dead.

However, we still watch and wait - just as the disciples did. We call this a "Vigil", and the Easter Vigil is the most important service in the Christian Church. It is celebrated on Holy Saturday evening, after dark.

A Paschal candle is lit from the Easter fire.

Activities

1. Imagine you are one of these five people who are mentioned in the Gospel accounts of Jesus' passion and death:

(i) Mary, his mother;

(ii) Peter, who denied he knew him;

(iii) Pontius Pilate, who condemned him;

(iv) the Roman soldier who described him as the Son of God;

(v) Nicodemus, who helped to bury him.

Describe your experience:

(a) What were you thinking about on the Saturday, the day after Jesus died?

(b) How did you spend the day?

(c) Recall some of the good times you had with Jesus, what were they?

(d) What impressed you most about him?

Research

2. There are several stages in the Easter Vigil; most of them are symbolic in some way. The simple acts demonstrate something far deeper.

(a) The service is held in the evening. Why do you think this is?

(b) It starts outside; the church is in total darkness. Read John 1:1-5.

(c) A fire is lit, and the priest lights a large candle from it. What is this candle called? Find out what is written on the candle and what each symbol means.

(d) It is carried into the dark church. What does the priest sing as he enters the church?

(e) We all light our smaller candles from the large candle. Why? (Matthew 5:14-16)

(f) We re-make the promises our parents and godparents made on our behalf at our baptisms. Find out what those promises were.

The Paschal Mystery

Activities

3. Write a simple explanation of the Easter Vigil for a younger pupil, explaining what the darkness represents, and how the candle overcomes it.

4. Complete the following sentence: "The resurrection of Jesus from the dead matters for me today because…"

5. Find the links between the Passover and the Last Supper. Copy this diagram into your exercise book. From the notices on the notice board below, choose the most appropriate to fill each of the blocks.

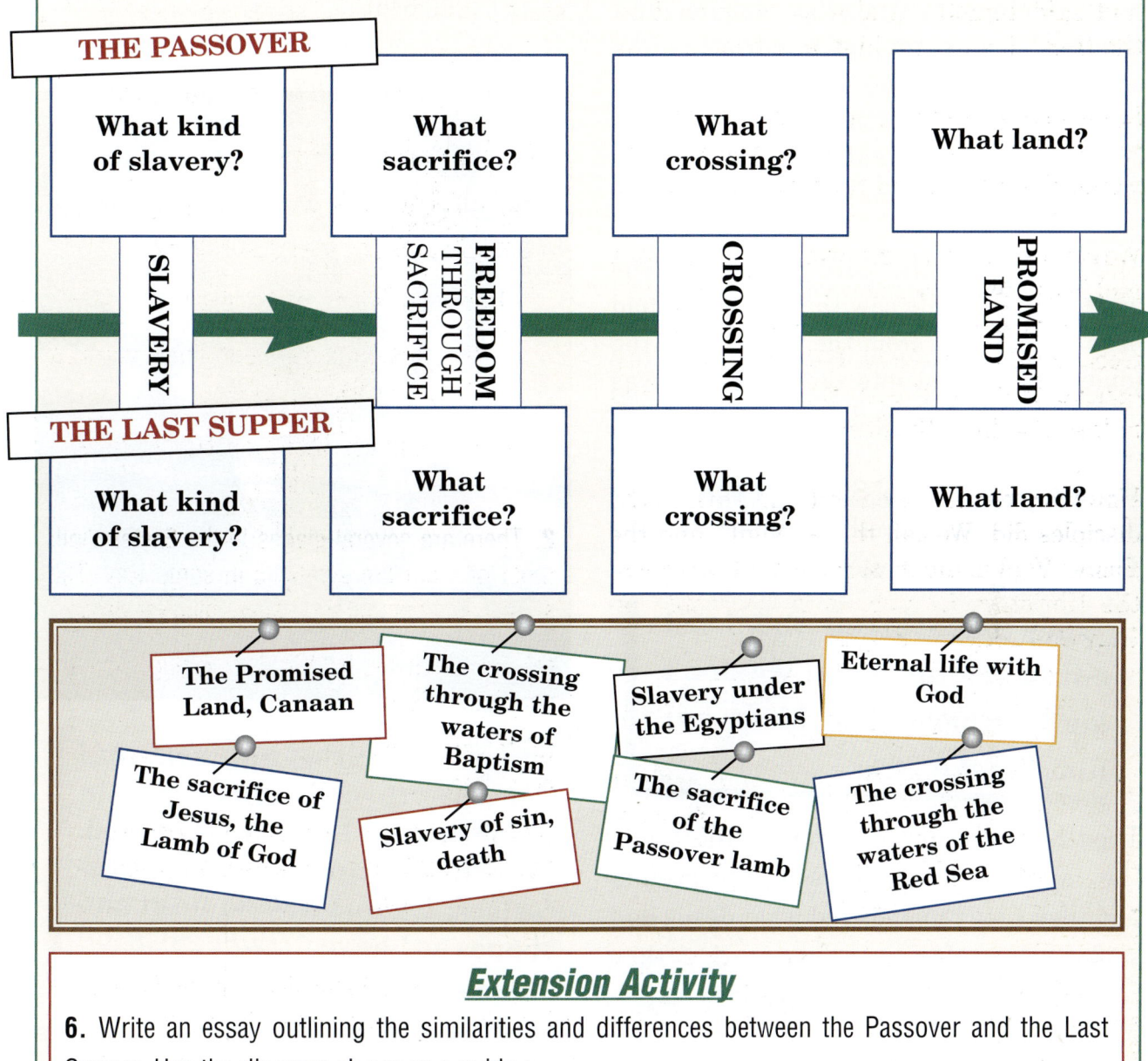

THE PASSOVER

| What kind of slavery? | What sacrifice? | What crossing? | What land? |

SLAVERY → FREEDOM THROUGH SACRIFICE → CROSSING → PROMISED LAND →

THE LAST SUPPER

| What kind of slavery? | What sacrifice? | What crossing? | What land? |

Notices:
- The Promised Land, Canaan
- The crossing through the waters of Baptism
- Slavery under the Egyptians
- Eternal life with God
- The sacrifice of Jesus, the Lamb of God
- Slavery of sin, death
- The sacrifice of the Passover lamb
- The crossing through the waters of the Red Sea

Extension Activity

6. Write an essay outlining the similarities and differences between the Passover and the Last Supper. Use the diagram above as a guide.

Glossary
VIGIL, SYMBOLIC.

The Paschal Mystery

The Resurrection

"He is not here: he is risen."

The Feast of Passover was over. The day of rest - the Sabbath - had passed. Dawn broke. Daylight started to fill the sky. People could once again resume their daily business.

Among the first to awake was Mary, a woman who had followed Jesus from her home in Magdala. And what was her first thought? I must go and finish attending to Jesus' body. When it was laid in the tomb on Friday afternoon, they had not completed the treatment that was required by Jewish Law.

She hurried to the garden. And as she went, she suddenly saw that the stone had been rolled away from the entrance of the tomb. She rushed into the tomb and was devastated to find that the body of Jesus was no longer there. The tomb was empty. Jesus' body was gone! She came running to Simon Peter and the other disciple, the one Jesus loved, and shouted:

> *"They have taken the Lord out of the tomb and we don't know where they have put him." (John 20:2)*

Then both the disciples ran to the tomb, they saw the linen cloths on the ground and then they remembered what Jesus had said to them. It was only now that they really understood what Jesus had been trying to explain to them:

> *"Till this moment they had failed to understand the teaching of scripture, that he must rise from the dead." (John 20:9)*

However, it was not simply a case of Jesus' body "disappearing".

> "Christ's Resurrection was not a return to earthly life.... In his risen body he passes from a state of death to another life beyond time and space." (CCC 646)

> *"Why are you so agitated, and why are these doubts rising in your hearts? Look, it is I indeed. Touch me and see for yourselves; a ghost has no flesh and bones as I have." (Luke 24:38-40)*

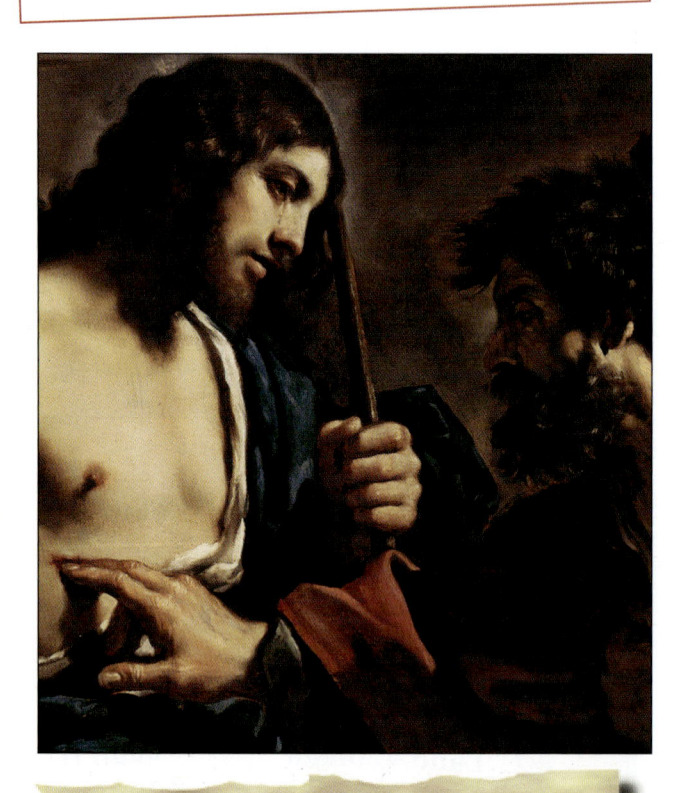

The writers of the Gospels list numerous occasions when Jesus - alive and real - appeared to his followers after the Resurrection: in the garden itself, in the Upper Room, on a road outside Jerusalem, at the Sea of Galilee... He talked with them and even ate with them.

The Paschal Mystery

Activities

1. Read John 20:1-18. Copy and complete the table for Easter Sunday.

EASTER SUNDAY

Gospel reference?	
What happened?	
Who was involved?	
Where did it happen?	

2. Mary Magdalene got a shock. List four possible explanations why Jesus' body was not in the tomb when she got there. Who might have moved it, and for what reason?

3. Imagine that you were present when Jesus appeared after the Resurrection; for example, you could be:

- Peter (John 21:1-18)
- Mary of Magdala (Luke 24:1-11)
- Cleopas (Luke 24:13-35)
- Thomas (John 20:19-29)
- Nathanael (John 21:1-17)

(a) Say who you are and what you were doing when Jesus appeared.

(b) What did Jesus say or do while you were present?

(c) What did you do as a result?

(d) What effect did it have upon your belief in Jesus and your life afterwards?

Extension

4. You are the same newspaper reporter who covered Jesus' arrival in Jerusalem and his crucifixion. Your editor has asked you for a news article for the Monday morning edition of the 'Jerusalem News'. What do you write?

You may find some useful pictures for your article using this web site:

Try: www.culham.ac.uk/Easter/index.html

5. Look at these four statements:

(a) "Death is final. The Resurrection is just a story made up by people who can't accept that."

(b) "By rising from the dead on Easter Sunday, Jesus provided the ultimate proof that there is life after death - and all of us share in it."

(c) "I don't know whether the Resurrection is true or not. OK, millions of people might believe in it, but it really doesn't make any difference to me today, does it?"

(d) "By his Cross and Resurrection, Christ has set us free. He is the Saviour of the world."

Identify which of these statements Christians believe, and give reasons for your answers.

> "The Resurrection of Jesus is the crowning truth of our faith in Christ." (CCC 638)

The Paschal Mystery

The Paschal Mystery

The Paschal Mystery is at the heart of Christian faith. This states that:

- Jesus died for our sins;
- Jesus rose from the dead;
- Jesus will come again.

> "Lord, by your cross and resurrection you have set us free. You are the saviour of the world." *(From the Mass)*

These beliefs had such a profound effect upon Jesus' followers that, shortly after the Resurrection, they devoted their lives entirely to telling people about Jesus. The Sabbath - the day of rest - was changed to Sunday, because that was the day on which Jesus rose from the dead. The disciples followed Jesus' instructions by celebrating the Eucharist together, sharing bread and wine and knowing that it had now become his Body and Blood.

Key points to remember

The empty tomb is a sign that death has been overcome. Jesus died that we might live. He laid down his life to show his love.

Because Jesus rose from the dead, death is not for us the end of the story, it is the beginning. There is life after death. It is life with God. The purpose of our present life is to prepare for that.

Glossary

THE UPPER ROOM, EUCHARIST.

5 The Prophetic Role of the Church

What is a prophet?

When God's way is not being followed, people need to be reminded about what is right and good, about what God wants. A person who does this is called a "Prophet"; he or she, through words or example, urges people to return to God's way.

A prophet is someone who speaks God's Word. In the Old Testament, we read about some people who were chosen by God and called to proclaim God's message or Word to the people.

Prophets of the Old Testament

God promised the Israelites (Jews) a blessed future without giving them precise details of how and when it would all happen. Many centuries were to pass before the promises were fulfilled. As a result, the people were often tempted to forget the story of their origin.

The people of Israel, unfortunately, did not live up to their side of the Covenant. They drifted into worshipping other gods. Rich Israelites oppressed poor Israelites. Instead of worshipping God wholeheartedly, people began to be 'two-faced' towards God, going through the motions of worship but not loving God from the heart. God did not abandon Israel. God did something else. He sent prophets. He filled them with his Word and told them to proclaim it to a sinful people.

These prophets called on the people to change their ways, to stop being unfair or worshipping false gods, and return to the way of life demanded by God, to be faithful to the Covenant. Their words were sometimes fierce and full of warning. But behind every word was love - the love that God still had for unfaithful Israel.

One of the most famous prophets, Isaiah.

If someone announces to a group of people 'Unless you change your way of life, you will all perish', he will not be seen as a very loving person.

Sometimes the prophets were told to be quiet and to stop upsetting people. But if their message was true, then their words were love. To say nothing and let people perish would have been to show far less love.

> "Woe... to those who refuse justice to the unfortunate and cheat the poor among my people of their rights."
> (Isaiah 10:1-2)

> "Come back to me, disloyal children - it is the Lord who speaks - for I alone am your Master." (Jeremiah 3:14)

The Prophetic Role of the Church

God's message proclaimed by the Prophets

The prophets knew that they had to remind people continually of their dependency on God. They did not rely on themselves, but had abundant trust in God. This trust in God helped them to keep going all the time. Even when the way ahead was very difficult, they knew God would never abandon them. Others might take advantage of them and mistreat them, even persecute them; human help might collapse and trusted friends let them down; but God would always be with them.

The prophets' message was fierce when they encountered people who believed that they had no need of God. They warned them of the danger of becoming absorbed in material things and forgetting all about the Ten Commandments. Pride, they proclaimed, left no room in a person's heart for God.

"Seek good and not evil so that you may live." (Amos 5:14)

"I will heal their disloyalty, I will love them with all my heart." (Hosea 14:5)

Activities

1. Write the word next to its correct definition:

Word	Definition
Prophet	What the Prophet must do
Prophecy	The words of a Prophet
Prophesy	A solemn friendship agreement with promises and duties
Covenant	One who hears God's Word and proclaims it

2. Prophets were often unwelcome because they had 'hard truths' to tell. What 'hard truths' do you think the world today needs to hear?

3. False prophets in Israel often told 'soft lies' (what people wanted to hear) and so were very popular.

For example, they proclaimed that peace and happiness were coming, when in fact trouble was approaching.

(a) Do you think people are being told 'soft lies' today?

(b) Where are these 'soft lies' coming from?

Amos

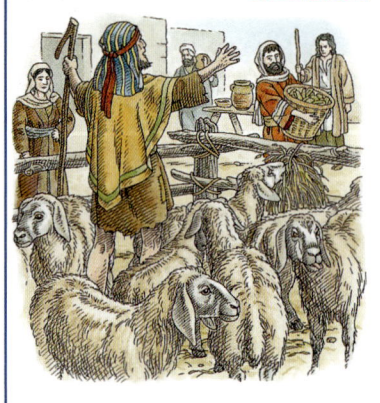

Amos was a shepherd, so he probably went to the main market towns to sell his sheep.

There he saw a lot of cheating going on: poor people being sold as slaves, judges accepting bribes, and rich people unwilling to help those worse off than themselves. He would have also watched people going to religious services but behaving badly the rest of the time. He knew that that was not enough: they had to lead a good life and behave justly as well. He kept pointing out that not caring for "the needy" is one of the main sins for which people would be punished.

Hosea

Hosea explained that what God seeks is a true religion of the heart:

> "What I want is love, not sacrifice, knowledge of God, not holocausts." *(Hosea 6:6)*

The marriage theme in Hosea is a symbol of the relationship between God and the Israelites. He describes the true covenant relationship of God with Israel. God is Israel's loving husband and, in response to his love and care, he expects faithful love in return. This is what the covenant bond demands - a true devotion of mind and heart.

Hosea described Israel's turning away from God as a married man with an unfaithful wife. Having married an unfaithful wife himself, he knew exactly how God felt about Israel's 'adultery'.

Jeremiah

Jeremiah was a very humble man, warm-hearted, very sensitive; he wanted to love and to be loved. Yet he knew that God wanted him to speak out and say what people would not want to hear. He knew this would make him unpopular with the people. He felt so helpless he cried out:

> "My grief is incurable, my heart within me is faint." *(Jeremiah 8:18)*

He pleaded day and night for God's help. He trusted completely in God and knew that with him all things are possible.

Isaiah

One of the greatest prophets of the Old Testament - many would say the greatest - was Isaiah. Like other prophets, he urged the people to improve their lives or risk punishment. But more importantly, he also expressed God's mercy and love. He looked ahead to the fulfilment of God's promises, and to a time when there would be no more pain and suffering, no more evil and injustice. He looked ahead to the coming of a Saviour or Messiah, and to the establishment of God's kingdom.

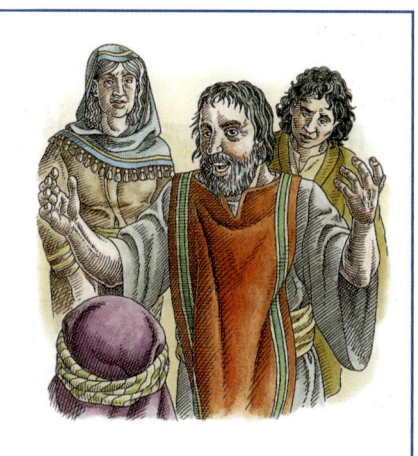

The Prophetic Role of the Church

Being a Follower of Jesus
Christians as today's prophets

Jesus told us that he would be with us always. The Church is a sign that the risen Jesus is present in the world. The Church is not a building made of wood and stone. Nor is it something out of date or out of touch, dead and lifeless.

Tens of thousands of people celebrate the Jubilee Year in Rome.

The Church is alive and growing. It is made up of living people.

WE ARE THE CHURCH. Through us, the risen Jesus lives and is active in the world.

WE ARE THE CHURCH. We are called to be "prophets", just as Jesus was a prophet.

WE ARE THE CHURCH. Like the prophets of the Old Testament, and like Jesus himself, we are called to speak out for:

- **JUSTICE** for the poor;
- **COMPASSION** for the weak;
- **REPENTANCE** (changed lives) among those who do wrong, and...
- **FAITHFULNESS** to God and to his commandments.

A disciple of Jesus is someone who hears Jesus' message, believes it and tries to live by it.

A disciple of Jesus is someone who is taught by Jesus and is willing to learn.

A disciple of Jesus is someone who wishes and tries to carry his message to others.

As disciples of Jesus, we are called:

- to spread the "good news" (see Luke 4:18-19);
- to tell others about Jesus;
- to help them to know him and love him;
- to make the world a happier and more just place, and...
- to guide others towards eternal joy with God.

The teachings of the Church touch every aspect of people's lives. Building on the Ten Commandments of the Old Testament and studying what Jesus said during his life on earth, it teaches how we relate to each other, help and love each other. The Church speaks out against war and violence. It strongly defends the rights and dignity of all human beings, especially the powerless or weak. It urges all people to be very conscious about the needs of the poor with regard to the use of resources and wealth.

Jesus has a unique relationship with God, the Father. That is why he was able to teach his disciples many things about life and love and God. We can find these important messages in the Bible and in the teachings of the Catholic Church.

The Prophetic Role of the Church

Activities

1. Look up these passages in the Gospels:

(a) Matthew 5:13-16; Salt of the earth and light of the world.

(b) Mark 8:34-38; Saving and losing one's life.

(c) Luke 18:18-30; The rich young man.

(d) John 13:12-17; Washing the disciples' feet.

2. Choose the Scripture passage you consider to be the most important for you. Think about it for a while, and then write an account of how your life might change if you were to put it fully into practice.

3. Work in pairs - make a list of the ways teenagers can help:

(a) elderly people;

(b) a person who is housebound;

(c) a mother with two or three small children;

(d) a priest who does not have enough young people to help him.

4. Choose one of the situations from the previous question and write down what you could do next week to help.

Extension

5. Jesus said:

> "I am the Way, the Truth and the Life." *(John 14:6)*

Work in groups of three to plan an assembly for the school.

You are to be the prophetic voice of Jesus. Choose practical examples from the lives of young people to show how the teaching and example of Jesus could give them inner peace and true happiness in life.

Glossary
COMPASSION.

The Prophetic Role of the Church

Go out to the world
The Church's teaching in action

There was once a group of twenty people in a restaurant. In the kitchen, the chef prepared twenty meals. The waiters and waitresses collected the meals from the kitchen, took them into the restaurant, and gave fifteen of them to five customers, so they enjoyed three meals each. The other fifteen customers had to share five meals - a mere third of a meal each!

How do you think the fifteen people felt?

This sort of injustice is happening all over the world today.

There is enough food to feed everyone. There are enough natural resources, education opportunities and health care for everyone. But they are not shared out evenly - one meal for each person. Instead, the people living in rich countries (known as the North or First World) are enjoying comfortable lives, while the 75% who live in poorer countries (known as the South or the Third World) often go hungry, are uneducated and suffer from diseases and preventable illnesses.

What can we, as Christians, do about this? For over 30 years, CAFOD has been working to help people in poor countries to help themselves, and also to change the unfair circumstances that lead to poverty and injustices in the first place. CAFOD is the overseas development and relief agency of the Catholic Church in England and Wales.

CAFOD supports over 1,000 projects and works in partnership with local people in Asia, Africa, Latin America and Eastern Europe to tackle poverty.

CAFOD helps people in the poorest countries of the world to help themselves.

In May 1999, Jon Sobrino, a Jesuit priest working in El Salvador, Central America, visited England and gave a talk to CAFOD supporters. Here are a few statistics that he included in his address:

> - "In 1996, around 365 people owned as much money or resources as maybe 45 or 48 poorest nations."
> - "Every year 35-40 million people die out of poverty".

> - "Over one sixth of the world's population, 1,300 million people, live on less than 1 dollar (60p) a day..."

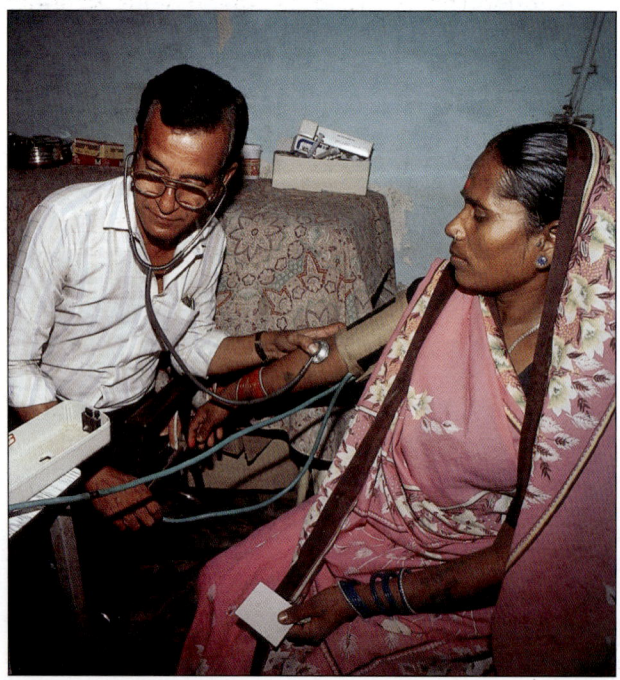

Medical care at work, Bombay, India.

The Prophetic Role of the Church

Activities

1. (a) Work out your daily expenses, try to include everything, cost of each meal, travel etc.

(b) Put yourself in the position of one of those 1,300,000,000 people that Father Sobrino referred to. Spend a few minutes thinking about it.

A CAFOD funded community development programme.

(c) Describe how you would survive? How would you live, eat, have clothes?

2. Visit CAFOD's website: www.cafod.org.uk.

3. Using the materials you get from the CAFOD website or other sources, compare the following facts/statistics about people living in a poor country in Africa, Asia or Latin America, and someone living in Britain.

(a) On average, how many years do people live?

(b) What percentage of the population goes to school?

(c) How many children die before the age of five, as a result of illness or lack of food?

(d) Find other evidence that demonstrates the difference between living conditions in Britain and a developing country.

4. CAFOD helps people in England and Wales to understand the causes of third world poverty and how to bring about change - through school programmes, youth work and parish groups. Describe any other area of work it undertakes.

5. Make contact with your Regional CAFOD office and find out how you can get involved in the work of CAFOD.

6. Suggest some ways in which your school might be able to contribute to CAFOD's work.

Extension

7. Do some research using the Internet, to find out about the richest people in a particular area of Britain. Then compare their wealth with the resources of the world's poorest nations. What do you think could be done to rectify this imbalance?

Glossary
THIRD WORLD.

The Prophetic Role of the Church

The Church's Teaching

Doing as Jesus commanded

The Church believes it is an essential part of our work as Christians to care for people, because Jesus said so. Over the centuries, the Church has taught that every individual is special. In a wide variety of documents and letters, the Church has spoken about the "development of peoples"; in other words, the rights and dignity of every human being. As Pope John Paul II put it:

"Whatever is opposed to life itself, ...whatever violates the integrity of the human person, ...whatever insults human dignity, ...all these things and others like them are infamies indeed. They poison human society... and they are a supreme dishonour to the Creator." (The Gospel of Life, 1995)

With so many people living in poverty in the world today, it would be easy for us to despair, to say there's nothing we can do about it. Especially for me personally: what can *I* do about it? I'm just one person, with no influence or power. How can *I* be a prophet for the poor and the rejected, those who suffer and are treated unjustly?

It is not only the famous prophets of the Old Testament who can call for a change in the way we live or in society. All of us have a responsibility as Christians - as disciples of Jesus - to be "prophets".

This is why Christians campaign and work on behalf of many in society who are poor, weak or unable to care for themselves for whatever reason. Organisations such as CHAS (the Catholic Housing Aid Society) help people find homes and achieve a decent level of accommodation. The Saint Vincent de Paul Society (SVP) is dedicated to reducing or eliminating poverty. Dioceses throughout England and Wales provide care for the elderly, for children, for people with handicaps, and others.

In parishes, individuals or small voluntary groups offer transport to people who are housebound, help young parents with small children, visit the sick or prisoners, or engage in a wide range of other activities. All of these small acts are examples of people putting into practice what Jesus taught us:

"A new commandment I give to you: that you love one another." (John 13:34)

A homeless person on the streets of London

"When someone steals another's clothes, we call them a thief. Should we not give the same name to one who could clothe the naked and does not? The bread in your cupboard belongs to the hungry; the coat hanging unused in your closet belongs to the one who needs it; the shoes rotting in your closet belong to the one who has no shoes; the money which you hoard up belongs to the poor." **(St. Basil)**

The Prophetic Role of the Church

Activities

1. Reflect on the words of St. Basil.

"When someone steals another's clothes, we call them a thief. Should we not give the same name to one who could clothe the naked and does not?"

Do you agree or disagree? Give reasons for your answer showing that you have considered more than one point of view.

2. Read the following story and write out the message you think it might have for each one of us.

A little fellow in the ghetto was teased by one who said, "If God loves you, why doesn't he take care of you? Why doesn't God tell someone to bring you shoes and a warm coat and better food?" The little lad thought for a moment then, with tears starting in his eyes, said: "I guess he does tell somebody, but somebody forgets."

Research

3. Find out about the work of one Catholic charity that operates in your area. Write an account of the work it does, giving specific examples of how it helps people.

4. Find out what is happening in your own parish, school or local area by way of initiatives to help the poor, the lonely, the sick and all who suffer injustice and see what you can do to join a group in order to help.

5. Plan a course of action to alert other students in the school to their duty to care for those in great need of our help.

(a) Make a collage of pictures (from newspapers/magazines or the Internet) showing poverty or other forms of injustice, whether from Britain or overseas.

(b) Use quotations from the teaching of Jesus in the Gospel and/or documents on Catholic Social Teaching.

Reference: The Busy Christian's Guide to Catholic Social Teaching.
Try: www.uscatholic.org/cstline/tline.html

(c) Select an area of the school corridor and get permission to mount a big display of your work.

(d) Organise some fund-raising activities in order to help a charity of your choice.

Key points to remember

"I was hungry and you gave me food; I was thirsty and you gave me a drink; I was a stranger and you made me welcome; naked and you clothed me .... I tell you solemnly, in so far as you did this to one of the least of these brothers or sisters of mine, you did it to me."
(Matthew 25:35 & 40)

Glossary
INTEGRITY, INFAMIES, CATHOLIC SOCIAL TEACHING.

The Prophetic Role of the Church

Modern Day Prophets
Life is full of opportunities

John Paul II

John Paul II.

"Along every step of the way I am moved by a vivid sense of God who has gone before us and leads us on, who wants us to honour him in spirit and in truth, to acknowledge the differences between us, but also to recognise in every human being the image and likeness of the One Creator of heaven and earth."

Those words are taken from the Opening Address given by Pope John Paul II on his historic visit to Israel in March 2000. In a modern sense, they sum up the message of the Old Testament prophets over 2,000 years ago.

Many would call Karol Wojtyla (his name before being elected Pope in 1978) a 20th Century prophet. In his travels and in his writings, he has striven to bring people closer to God, has called them to repentance and has urged them to consider their special relationship with God. Over and over again he has proclaimed the dignity of the human person, especially the dignity and rights of the unborn and the duty of wealthy societies to act generously towards refugees and immigrants. He continuously appeals for peace and, between 1995-2000, he has protested against the violence of war over three hundred times.

Mother Teresa

Mother Teresa.

Jesus said, "I was hungry and you gave me food; I was thirsty and you gave me to drink... in so far as you did this to one of the least of these brothers and sisters of mine, you did it to me...".

"The least of these brothers and sisters of mine"- the lepers, the poor, the destitute- these were the very people among whom Mother Teresa made her life's work, the very people our Lord was speaking of in St Matthew's Gospel. And to her dying day, they simply called her "Mother".

For 50 years, Mother Teresa devoted her life to those she found lying in the gutters - dirty, starving, disease-ridden people, robbed of their dignity by the circumstances of their lives. She became a symbol of hope among the hopeless.

On a visit to Edinburgh in 1993, she spoke of finding a man on the streets of Calcutta who was "eaten up with worms". She took him in and cared for him. She gave him back his dignity. And before he died he told her: "I have lived like a dog, but I shall die like an angel". That was her gift. She cared passionately. She gave of her whole life in the service of the Lord - through serving the least of his brothers and sisters.

(Bishop Vincent Logan preaching at a Requiem Mass for Mother Teresa.)

The Prophetic Role of the Church

Jean Vanier

Jean Vanier is often described as a modern day prophet - as a man of "vision". He puts the Gospel into action, as when our Lord spoke about inviting... "the poor, the crippled, the lame and the blind" to share good things, not simply the rich and the healthy." (cf. Luke 14:12-14).

Jean Vanier.

Jean Vanier spent some time in the Marines and travelled a lot. While he was in France he was introduced to various lay Christian communities. He spent time in prayer and reflection and was soon convinced that God was calling him to establish a lay community for people with intellectual disabilities. He believed they were among the loneliest and most rejected in the world. He knew that the weak and the vulnerable were very dear to Jesus' heart. Some of them felt rejected by society because they were "different", but to Jean, they were "special".

He bought an old ruined house and called it L'Arche (The Ark). It opened on 5 August 1964 and became a warm, loving community for "special" people. In a short time, he opened other L'Arche communities. There are now 117 of them in 33 different countries worldwide, spreading from Canada to the Ivory Coast, from India to Honduras, and from Great Britain to Haiti.

Each L'Arche is a witness of God's love and care for those who are rejected or in pain. People no longer feel lonely because they are loved. They lead a very simple life: eating, working and praying together with time for celebrating and welcoming visitors.

Jean Vanier's vision was that the communities of L'Arche and the others he founded should be places where the gospel message is lived out, where people - no matter how handicapped or disadvantaged - should feel they were in the presence of Jesus, surrounded by others (a community) and the love of God. Most of all, they should be a place of "welcome":

> "Whoever welcomes one of these little ones in my name, welcomes me." *(Luke 9:48)*

75

The Prophetic Role of the Church

Dorothy Day

Dorothy Day.

Her Catholic faith led her and others to open Houses of Hospitality across America where poor people could come for meals, clothes and accommodation. She also campaigned for improved rights for workers, and helped start the Catholic Workers Movement.

At the age of fourteen, Dorothy Day walked around the streets of West Chicago in the USA and witnessed at first hand the conditions in which people were living. Their homes were slums; they had little food or clothing. At first she became angry and thought of helping them through political action.

Later, Dorothy believed that God wanted her to help these people in a different way.

She did not know how, but she prayed about it. She was convinced of God's continuing promise to us that he is with us always, with his comforts and joy, if only we will ask.

The poor during the American depression queuing outside one of the soup kitchens of 'The Catholic Workers Movement'.

"The mystery of the poor is this: that they are Jesus, and what you do for them you do for him. It is the only way we have of knowing and believing in our love. The mystery of poverty is that by sharing in it, making ourselves poor in giving to others, we increase our knowledge of and belief in love".
(From Selected Writings)

"Christ has no body now on earth but yours. Yours are the only hands with which he can do his work... Yours are the only eyes through which his compassion can shine upon a troubled world. Christ has no body now on earth but yours." (St Teresa of Avila)

The Prophetic Role of the Church

Archbishop Oscar Romero

Most of the wealth in the Central American country of El Salvador is held by just a handful of families. The majority of the population of over five million live in extreme poverty; they barely have enough food to stay alive. Their homes consist of cardboard boxes or corrugated sheeting, without water or electricity. In the 1970s, priests who spoke on their behalf were often tortured or murdered.

When Oscar Romero became Archbishop of El Salvador in 1977, he came to realise the extent of the people's misery and recognised the corruption and evil of the political regime. He was determined to preach for the rights of the poor, Saying: "The world that the Church must serve is the world of the poor."

The authorities were worried and angry that he not only spoke out for the impoverished and persecuted people of El Salvador, but he even broadcast criticism of the government. He was silenced by an assassin's bullet as he celebrated Mass in March 1980.

Archbishop Oscar Romero.

Activities

Investigate the life and work of a modern day prophet. You can use one of the above or choose another. Write an account of their life, explaining how the Gospel motivated their actions or teachings, and why they could be described as "prophets".

For further information on some of the modern day prophets mentioned:
Try: www.silk.net/RelEd/teresa.html
Try: www.larche.org.uk

- Be clear about what information you need.

(a) What country did this person live in?

(b) What did (s)he do?

(c) What difference did this person make to the lives of other people?

(d) What was the reaction of others?

(e) What sacrifices did this person make?

(f) In what way were they following the teachings of Jesus?

- Be able to make a judgement on your prophet.

(g) How can you say this person is a prophet today?

(h) What do you think of their life?

(i) What lessons can be learnt from their life?

- Decide how you are going to present your information and judgement to the rest of the class so that you can make your points clearly and in an interesting way.

The Prophetic Role of the Church

Key points to remember
Meditation

Jesus called to him his twelve disciples and gave them authority over unclean spirits, to cast them out, and to heal every disease and infirmity...

"Go to the lost sheep of Israel, and preach as you go, saying: 'The kingdom of heaven is at hand'. Heal the sick, raise the dead, cleanse lepers, cast out demons. You received without paying, give without pay. Take no gold, nor silver, nor copper in your belts, no bag for your journey, nor two tunics, nor sandals, nor a staff; for the labourer deserves his food... Behold, I send you out as sheep in the midst of wolves; so be wise as serpents and innocent as doves. Beware of men, for they will deliver you up to councils, and flog you in their synagogues, and you will be dragged before governors and kings for my sake, to bear witness before them and the Gentiles. When they deliver you up, do not be anxious how you are to speak or what you are to say; for what you are to say will be given to you in that hour; for it is not you who speak, but the Spirit of your Father speaking through you".
(Matthew 10:1, 5-10, 16-20)

With those words, Jesus sent out his disciples on their first mission. The message today is similar for all who wish to follow Jesus.

We are to help cure the ills, the diseases, of society - poverty and injustice - and proclaim the good news and new life.

We need to have total faith in God, not worrying about material things, but witnessing to others through our lives that loving God is more important than anything else.

God's love and care for us is boundless, and he will never let us down. So even when the going gets tough - even if we were to face torture and death like Oscar Romero or the prophets of the Old Testament - we should never fear.

This is the mission of the prophet. This is the mission of the Church. This is OUR mission as disciples of Jesus.

Glossary
LAY PEOPLE, GENTILES, SYNAGOGUE, REFUGEE, MISSION.

6 The Church in Britain

"Go out to the whole world, proclaim the Good News to all creation."

After the Resurrection, Jesus instructed his disciples to go out to the whole world; to proclaim the Good News to all creation (Mark 16:15). The disciples set out on a journey of faith. Their story is one of excitement, adventure, bravery, selflessness and love. It is our story too, for through our Baptism, we are called to join this journey of faith.

We are surrounded in our everyday lives by the symbols and signs of our rich Catholic past, for example: churches, street names, hospitals, festivals, paintings, books and place names. There are many reasons for this, which we will explore in this chapter.

Christianity came to Britain soon after the death and Resurrection of Jesus, because both Israel and Britain were part of the Roman Empire. So our story begins in Roman Britain that was part of a multi-cultural, multi-ethnic empire stretching from Asia Minor in the east, to the northern borders with Scotland. The various religions, including Christianity, travelled with the Roman army to all corners of the known world.

A fourth century British Roman mosaic depicting Christ.

At this time, those in positions of power saw Christianity as a threat. Why?

The Romans worshipped many gods and even considered their Emperor to be a god. To refuse to accept this was seen as treason.

It became very dangerous to be a Christian. Christians had to live their faith in secret, but they still continued to spread the Good News wherever and whenever they could. Many men, women and children from these communities throughout the Empire were persecuted and killed for their faith: they were the early martyrs.

> "I ask them if they are Christians. If they do not admit it, I repeat the question a second and third time, threatening them with capital punishment. If they persist, I sentence them to death... For whatever kind of crime they have committed, they are so obstinate that they should certainly be punished."
> (Pliny, a Roman Governor)

The Church in Britain

The First British Martyr

The first known Christian martyr in Britain was Alban.

St. Alban

The hour was late and Alban, a British soldier in the Roman army, was on the point of going to bed. The faint creak of the door leading into the courtyard of his villa, followed by the sound of whispering caught his attention. Curious to know who could be calling at that time of night, Alban walked quietly towards the door, where, to his surprise, he saw one of his slaves talking to an elderly man. On seeing his master, the slave started back in terror, but the stranger moved quietly between the two men and faced Alban, who demanded to know what was going on.

The man gave his name as Amphibalus and throwing himself on the mercy of Alban explained that he was a Christian priest who had fled from the town because he would not offer incense to the Emperor. He begged for shelter for the night. Alban listened in astonishment. He had heard of the Christians, but could not understand why they were so stubborn in their refusal to give worship to the Emperor. He decided to question the man further in the morning, before handing him over to the governor. The next day the priest was brought to Alban and he began to talk about his belief in Jesus. Over the next few days, Alban and the priest spent many hours talking and Alban came to know and believe in Jesus. Although it was very dangerous to give shelter to Christians, Alban found that he could not hand the priest over to the governor to be tortured and killed.

Then, without warning, soldiers arrived at the villa. Alban hurriedly put on the priest's clothes. He was then promptly arrested and dragged before the governor.

On discovering that the priest had escaped, the governor was furious and demanded that Alban should immediately offer incense to the Emperor to prove that he was still loyal to Roman beliefs, or suffer death. Alban declared, "I am called Alban and I worship and adore the true and living God who created all things".

Alban refused to betray his new found faith in Jesus, and after being tortured, was taken to the hill outside the town. His courage and faith so impressed one of the executioners that he too begged to be allowed to die for Jesus. The two men were beheaded and their witness of faith led many others to become Christians. A Church was eventually built on the site and it became a shrine and a centre of pilgrimage. A monastery was founded there and the town of St. Albans grew up around it.

The Church in Britain

Activities

1. Choose words from the box to finish the story of St. Alban.

Alban was a _____ in the Roman army. He did not know about Jesus. It was dangerous to be a _____. Christians were killed because they would not _____ the Roman gods. Alban hid a _____ in his house. The priest told Alban about _____. Then _____ understood and he became a Christian. When the soldiers came to _____ the priest, Alban put on the priest's _____. He was taken to the _____. The governor was angry when he found out what Alban had done. Alban would not give up believing in Jesus. He said "I am called Alban and I worship and _____ the true and living _____." He was put to _____. When people saw Alban's _____ many of them became _____ too. The place where Alban was _____ soon became a _____.
A shrine is a place where people come to pray and remember someone who was holy.

Word Bank: adore, Jesus, priest, arrest, God, faith, soldier, Alban, Christians, worship, death, martyred, shrine, clothes, Christian, governor

2. Why was it so difficult to be a Christian during the time of Alban?

3. Why did the Romans persecute Christians at that time?

4. How did Alban become involved with Christian teaching?

5. Why didn't Alban hand the priest over to the governor?

6. How did Alban first show that he had accepted the teachings of Jesus?

7. Why do you think Alban was prepared to die rather than give in to the threats of the Roman governor? In your answer think of the words of Jesus:

> "I am the Way, the Truth and the Life." *(John 14:6)*

Point to Note: Remember that years are numbered from the birth of Christ; A.D. (Anno Domini) means: 'The Year of Our Lord'. B.C. stands for 'Before Christ'.

Glossary
MULTI-CULTURAL, MULTI-ETHNIC, TREASON, PERSECUTED, EARLY MARTYRS.

The Church in Britain

How present day divisions among Christians arose
Henry VIII and the break from Rome

By the beginning of the 16th century, Europe was torn by wars of a political and religious nature. There was change everywhere. This also affected the Church in Britain. The Pope in Rome was head of the Roman Catholic Church in England as well as throughout the world. King Henry VIII was loyal to the Pope. He had no sympathy with the attacks on the Church by Martin Luther, the founder of Protestantism in Germany. If you look at any British coin you will see, on the 'heads' side, the letters F.D. or Fid. Def. These stand for *Fidei Defensor* which means Defender of the Faith. This title was given to Henry by the Pope in 1521 for writing a book *'Defence of the Seven Sacraments'*, against Luther's idea that there were only two sacraments - Baptism and the Lord's Supper.

Catherine of Aragon.

By the late 1520s, however, Henry's feelings were changing towards the Pope. In 1509 he had married Catherine of Aragon, a Spanish princess. They had one surviving child, a daughter, Mary. Henry was desperate for a son to succeed him but, following several unsuccessful pregnancies, Catherine seemed unable to provide him with one. So Henry decided to ask for an annulment of his marriage from the Pope, and to marry Anne Boleyn with whom he had fallen in love.

Anne Boleyn.

For Catholics, a marriage can be declared null (that means not truly a marriage) only if there are good reasons, which prove that the marriage was flawed from its very beginnings. In the teaching of Christ, a valid marriage lasts for a lifetime. In Henry's case, the decision to annul his marriage could only be made under the authority of the Pope. The Pope was not willing to declare Henry VIII's marriage null, as there were no reasons to do so. As a result, relations between the Pope and Henry grew worse. Henry, ignoring the Church, divorced Catherine and married Anne; they had a daughter, Elizabeth.

King Henry VIII.

The Church in Britain

In 1533 Henry began the break away from the Catholic Church by a series of Acts of Parliament. One such Act, the Act of Supremacy, declared Henry to be 'the Supreme Head of the Church in England'.

Some people were so horrified by Henry's actions that they opposed him by refusing to take the Oath of Supremacy. They were thrown into prison, prepared to endure torture and death rather than deny their conscience.

There are many martyrs from this period: two of the most famous are Sir Thomas More and Bishop John Fisher.

St. Thomas More, King Henry VIII's Lord Chancellor and now Patron Saint of Politicians.

Thomas More, Henry's Lord Chancellor, resigned because he firmly opposed Henry's plans to divorce Catherine and his views on papal supremacy. By resigning, he lost most of his income and lived in relative poverty, in comparison with his earlier lifestyle.

On 14 April 1534, Thomas More was summoned to Lambeth to take the Oath before the King's commissioners. He refused and was sent to the Tower of London, accused of treason. For over a year he could not be persuaded or bribed to change his mind. In July 1535, he was found guilty of treason and sentenced to be hanged, drawn and quartered at Tyburn, although King Henry changed the sentence to beheading on Tower Hill.

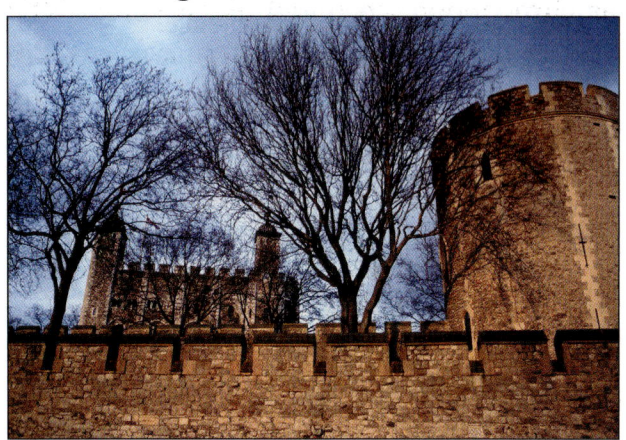

The Tower of London where St. Thomas More was imprisoned.

On the scaffold Thomas More declared:

"I die the King's good servant, but God's first".

Sir Thomas More died on 6 July 1535 and was canonised in 1935.

John Fisher, Bishop of Rochester.

John Fisher was the Bishop of Rochester and he also refused to take the oath. He was sent to the Tower of London on 26 April 1534. A year later, Pope Paul III honoured him by making him a cardinal, but Henry forbade the red hat - the symbol of the cardinal's position - to be brought into England; he was so angry that he declared he would send Fisher's head to Rome instead.

The Church in Britain

Return to the Catholic Church or be punished

When Edward died in July 1553, Henry VIII's daughter by Catherine of Aragon, Mary, succeeded the throne. Mary was a devout Catholic. Catholic bishops were re-instated and the doctrines of the Catholic Church were taught once more. Protestants who did not wish to live under Catholic rule were free to leave the country.

Mary I was determined to re-establish the Catholic Church in England, but many objected to it. As a consequence, around 300 Protestant men and women were burned at the stake, and many more were imprisoned and executed for their faith. Mary reigned for five turbulent years. People had now been forced to take sides: either Catholic or Protestant.

Mary died in 1558 and her half sister, Elizabeth I, became queen. She formulated an Anglican Settlement and fashioned the legal basis of the Church of England. She took the title of 'Supreme Governor of the Realm in Matters Spiritual and Temporal'. The thirty-nine Articles defining Anglican belief were published.

Queen Mary I.

Time-line of the Kings & Queens of England

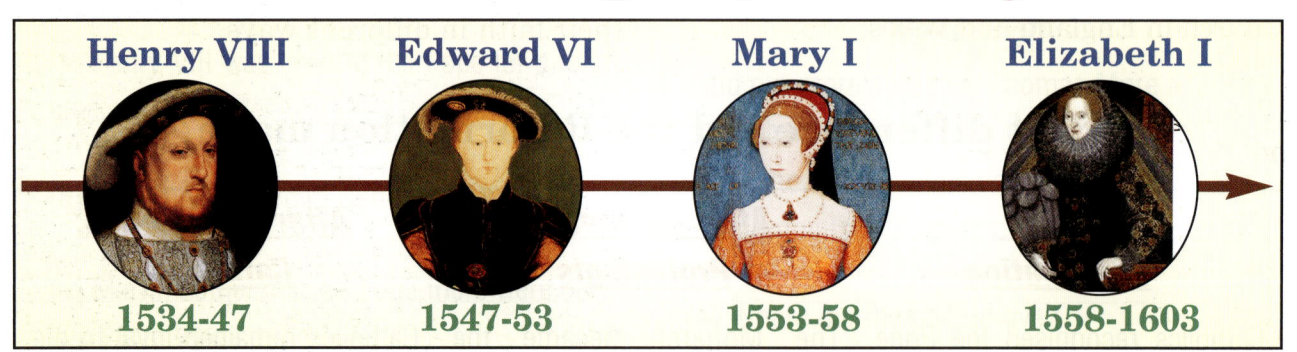

Henry VIII	Edward VI	Mary I	Elizabeth I
1534-47	1547-53	1553-58	1558-1603

Conform to the Church of England or be punished

In Queen Elizabeth I's reign, two Acts of Parliament, in 1559, called The Act of Supremacy and The Act of Uniformity, gave the monarch full authority over the Church of England and required all people to conform to it.

Elizabeth I of England.

In 1570, the Pope excommunicated Elizabeth and the rift between Rome and England was going to be long lasting and severe.

Punishments for those refusing to give up their Catholic Faith

(i) If a person spoke against the new religion:
- they would be fined £700 the first time;
- £2,800 the second time;
- their goods and possessions would all be confiscated if they persisted in criticising the Church of England.

(ii) Everyone was expected to attend the Sunday service in his or her parish church. If they didn't, they would be fined a shilling (5p), which was a day's wages for a skilled worker.

(iii) In 1563, Parliament introduced the death penalty for anyone convicted a second time of refusing to accept that the Queen was the Supreme Governor of the Church.

The Church in Britain

About 80% of the population conformed to the Church of England, to avoid the fines or other punishments. Those who remained loyal to the Catholic Church included about 500 priests. They either led a life of secrecy or fled abroad.

Catholic priests being pulled through the streets of London on a cart.

Over 300 Catholics, 123 of whom were priests, were executed during the reign of Elizabeth. The first priest-martyr in this period was Cuthbert Maine. He was pulled behind a cart to the place of execution. There he was hanged. He was cut down while still alive and then torn open and his bowels drawn out of him. Finally he was cut into four parts. This was a particularly gruesome form of execution known as being 'hanged, drawn and quartered' and was reserved for those found guilty of treason.

The gruesome form of execution in which the victim was 'hanged drawn and quartered'.

Catholic priests were not allowed to celebrate Mass or preach in England, but some worked secretly. If they were caught, they could be tortured and executed. This is what one of them - Fr. Edmund Campion - wrote in 1580:

"In the house where I am, all the talk is of death, fleeing, prison or the ruin of friends; yet they keep going with courage... Nor will this (Catholic) Church fail... Rumours of approaching danger force me to end this letter here."

Edmund Campion.

Edmund Campion was right to fear for his life. A year later, in 1581, he was captured. On December 1 he was dragged behind a horse to Tyburn Hill in London and there hanged, drawn and quartered.

Despite the dangers, many Catholic families took great risks to hide Catholic priests and built secret compartments in their homes where priests could hide to escape detection. These were known as 'priest holes'.

The Church in Britain

Father William Weston hid in one when what he called the 'heretics' burst into the house where he had been saying Mass:

> "From my cave-like hide, I could follow their movements by the noise and uproar they raised. Step by step, they drew closer, and when they entered my room, the sight of my books was an added incentive to their search. In that room there was also a secret passage for which they demanded the key, and as they opened the door onto it, they were standing immediately above my head. I could hear practically every word they said. 'Here, look!' they called out. 'A chalice! And a missal!' Then they demanded a hammer and other tools to break through the wall and panelling. They were certain now that I could not be far away..."

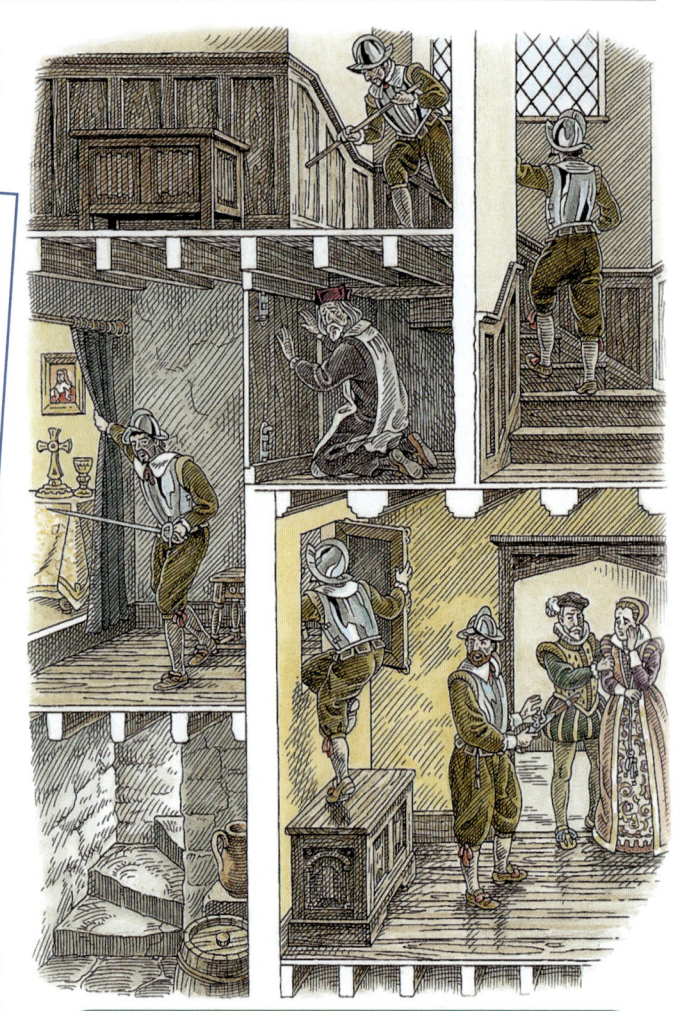

Fr. John Gerard SJ described how he was once cornered in a house and had to remain literally holed up in a wall for four days without food or water while a team tore up the floorboards and stripped the plaster off the walls around him.

Margaret Clitherow was one of the very courageous women who offered shelter to fugitive priests, hiding them in a special room where she and other secret Catholics could attend Mass.

Margaret Clitherow.

Activities

1. Match Column **A** with Column **B**

COLUMN A	COLUMN B
(i) Who was the monarch who followed Henry VIII?	(a) Mary I
(ii) What did the Book of Common Prayer replace?	(b) Elizabeth I
(iii) Which Church did Mary I belong to?	(c) Edward VI
(iv) Who was the queen who persecuted Protestants?	(d) The Missal
(v) Who was the queen who persecuted Catholics?	(e) Catholic

Activities

2. If you had been alive during the Reformation and a priest seeking refuge knocked at your door, what would you have done? Why?

3. The priests risked their lives and the lives of others.

(a) Why do you think they took these risks? Think about what would happen if:

- there were no priests,
- there were no sacraments,
- there was nobody to hear confessions,
- there was no Mass.

(b) In your opinion, what was the best thing for the priests to have done? Why?

Preparation for Group Work

4. Margaret Clitherow was an ordinary wife and mother who became a martyr for her faith. Read an account of her life. It can be found on *www.tere.org* in the section on 'Support Material'.

Group Work

5. Work in Groups:

(a) Discuss the aspects of Margaret Clitherow's character that you admire and then look at aspects that you do not agree with.

On your own:

(b) In bullet point form, show how Margaret Clitherow's life demonstrates the problems that ordinary people had to face during that time.

6. Choose one of the saints during the period of the Reformation, for example, Margaret Clitherow, Edmund Campion, John Southworth, Ambrose Barlow. Write Chapter 3 of your history of the Church. You should include the following:

- Short introduction describing what it was like to be a Catholic at this time;
- Your reason for choosing this particular person;
- What this person did.

7. Organise a class debate taking one of the Reformation saints you have studied. The motion should be:

"This person could have done more for the Church if he/she had been able to escape and remain free."

Research

8. Find out if there were:

(a) Catholics from your area martyred during the Reformation;

(b) houses in your area which hid Catholic priests, at this time, maybe with a 'priest hole'; or...

(c) places locally where either Protestants or Catholics were executed because of their faith.

Write down your findings.

Glossary

MISSAL, LITURGY, PROTESTANT, SPIRITUAL, TEMPORAL, PRIEST HOLES, HERETICS, CHALICE, SJ, EXCOMMUNICATED.

The Church in Britain

Emancipation

It was almost 200 years before Catholics in Britain were able to practise their Faith freely again, without fear of persecution. By the end of the 18th Century, there were very few of them left; they had very little influence in State affairs or politics, and were no longer seen as a threat.

Cardinal John Henry Newman.

John Henry Newman (1801-1890) was originally an Anglican (a member of the Church of England). But he became a Roman Catholic in 1845, and went on to be made a Cardinal. He described what it was like for Catholics at that time:

"No longer the Catholic Church in the country; nay, no longer, I may say, a Catholic community, but a few adherents of the Old Religion, moving silently and sorrowfully about, as memorials of what had been.

There, perhaps, an elderly person, seen walking in the streets, grave and solitary, and strange though noble in bearing, and said to be of goodly family, and a "Roman Catholic". An old-fashioned house of gloomy appearance closed in with high walls, with an iron gate, and yews, and the report attaching to it that "Roman Catholics" lived there; but who they were, and what they did, or what was meant by calling them Roman Catholics, no one could tell - though it had an unpleasant sound, and told of form and superstition."

The Relief Acts of 1778 and 1791, and the Emancipation Act (1829), allowed Catholics almost total freedom.

Benefits to Catholics from the passing of the Emancipation Act

- It was no longer illegal to be a Catholic. They didn't need to fear arrest or punishment.

- Catholics were allowed to build churches and worship in them.

- They were allowed to vote.

- They were allowed to stand as Members of Parliament. Five Catholic MPs were elected in the General Election of 1830.

- The Roman Catholic Church could run its own affairs, without interference from the State.

The Church in Britain

The number of Catholics began to grow until, in 1850, Rome decided that England and Wales could once again be divided into dioceses with a bishop in each one.

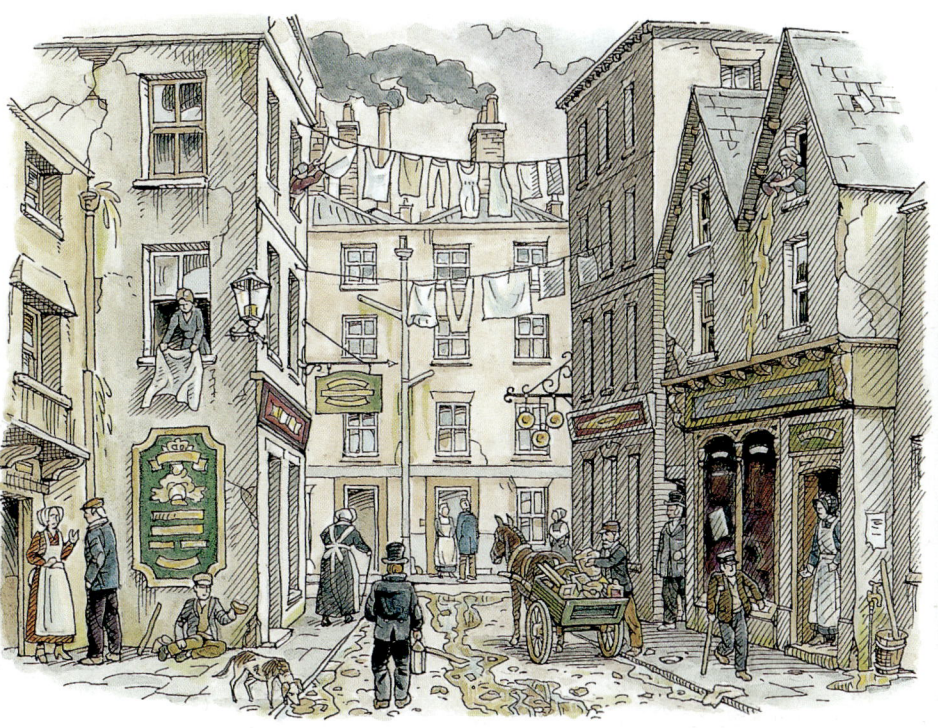

Cardinal Nicholas Wiseman.

Nicholas Wiseman was the first Archbishop of Westminster to be appointed. He made it clear that the Catholic Church would not be a threat to government or politics, but that it would condemn the appalling conditions that some people lived in:

> "The labyrinth of lanes and courts, and alleys and slums, nests of ignorance, vice, depravity, and crime, as well as of squalor, wretchedness and disease; whose atmosphere is typhus, whose ventilation is cholera; in which swarms a huge and countless population, in great measure, nominally at least, Catholic; haunts of filth, which no sewage committee can reach, dark corners, which no lighting boards can brighten..."

Activities

1. Today in England, we are able to practise our faith, free from fear of persecution. Imagine that a regime opposed to Christianity took over and you were not allowed to practise.

(a) What would change for you and your family?

(b) What difference would it make to your life?

2. Write Chapter 4 of your story of the history of the Church in England. The title should be 'Emancipation'.

Research

3. There are still restrictions on Catholics in England today in relation to the government and the monarchy. Find out at least two of them.

Glossary
EMANCIPATION, ADHERENTS, SUPERSTITION.

The Church in Britain

Christians Divided

JESUS CHRIST
The Church of Christ:
One, Holy,
Catholic, Apostolic.
PETER
Head of the Church.
POPE
Successor of St. Peter.

THE CHURCH OF ENGLAND
King Henry VIII began the split with Rome and the Church of England was established during the reign of Queen Elizabeth I.

THE SALVATION ARMY
William Booth and his wife Catherine founded it in London on 1865.

THE PENTECOSTAL CHURCH
Founded in the 1890s by a member of the American Bible Society.

METHODISM
This movement was started in the 18th century by John Wesley, an Anglican clergyman.

Activities

1. In Britain today, many people belong to different Churches. Prepare a statement saying which Church you belong to and why. If it is not the Catholic Church, try to find out some details about your Church so that you can share it with the rest of the class.

2. In what way is the Catholic Church, One, Holy, Catholic and Apostolic? (See Student's Book THE WAY, page 89.)

Pairwork

3. Choose another Church or Faith Community in your local area to study. Find out:

   (a) How it originated?

   (b) Who the founder was?

   (c) What is the main form of worship?

   (d) What sacraments does it recognise?

   (e) What are some of the main beliefs?

The Second Vatican Council

Jesus established One, Holy, Catholic and Apostolic Church to proclaim, develop and safeguard the truth until he comes again on the last day.

It is part of Catholic belief that all these gifts of God are to be found in the visible Catholic Church. It is also part of Catholic belief that many aspects of these gifts are to be found among baptised Christians in other Churches and denominations. As Catholics, we accept that members of the Church make mistakes, we belong to a Church of sinners, we can learn from other Christians and from other religions.

> Where there are sins, there are also divisions, schisms, heresies, and disputes. Where there is virtue, however, there also are harmony and unity, from which arise the one heart and one soul of all believers. (CCC 817)

The Second Vatican Council.

In the last century, in order to update the Catholic Church, Pope John XXIII called for a Council of the Church: the Second Vatican Council. It lasted for four years, from 1962 to 1965. The Council brought together 2,500 bishops from every continent in the world to reform and renew the Church.

Some highlights of the Second Vatican Council:

- The liturgy has been modernised, and the language of the people may replace Latin in the Mass and other services.

- Lay people are encouraged to play a greater role in the Church.

- The Council states clearly that the Catholic Church rejects nothing of those things which are true and holy in other religions.

- It states that everyone who is properly baptised and sincerely "seeks the truth" belongs to Christ - not just Catholics.

- It recognises that Christ died for all people, so those who belong to other faiths and sincerely follow non-Christian traditions can also be saved.

We are all parts of the "Body of Christ" to which St. Paul referred.

The Church in Britain

What is special about the Catholic Church?

What is exceptional about the Catholic Church is that it can trace its origins back *directly* to Christ through the apostles, in a way that the other denominations cannot. What Jesus founded is known as the Church of Christ, and we say that the Church of Christ "subsists" (continues to exist) within the Catholic Church. It is "one, holy, catholic and apostolic", and the Pope is the successor of St. Peter.

Pope John Paul II.

> "You are Peter and on this rock I will build my church, and the powers of death shall not prevail against it. I will give you the keys of the kingdom of heaven, and whatever you bind on earth shall be bound in heaven, and whatever you loose on earth shall be loosed in heaven."
> *(Matthew 16: 18 & 19)*

Other Christian denominations, while respecting the Pope, do not accept him as being the leader of all Christians. However, that does not stop them co-operating with the Catholic Church in other areas.

> Just as a human body, though it is made up of many parts, is a single unit because all these parts, though many, make one body, so it is with Christ.
> *(1 Corinthians 12:12)*

The Pope is a bishop - the Bishop of Rome. He has a special role in defining the teaching of the Church and applying it to the lives of Christians today. In this he works with all the other bishops of the Catholic Church. Together, they seek the truth as taught in the Bible and in the traditions that have been passed down over the past 2,000 years. On rare occasions, on matters of faith or morals, the Pope will make a pronouncement that is binding and unquestionably true. This is what is meant by the Pope being "infallible".

Together, all Christians strive to make the world a better, fairer place. We are united and motivated by our faith in God, and in his Son, Jesus Christ. We believe in the power of the Holy Spirit constantly to create and renew the Church. We pray for unity as Jesus instructed us:

> "That all may be one. As you, Father, are in me and I am in you, may they also be one in us, ...so that the world may know that you have sent me."
> *(John 17:21)*

The Church in Britain

One of the most important events in the journey towards Christian unity was the visit of Pope John Paul II to Britain in May and June 1982 - the first Pope ever to visit this country.

Cardinal Basil Hume described the Pope's visit in this way:

> "It was for other Christians much more than the confirmation of the movement towards Christian unity. Pope John Paul caused profound satisfaction, delight and some astonishment by his ecumenical sensitivity, his sureness of touch, and the obvious rapport between himself and the British Christians who welcomed him so generously."

For us, the message is clear: Jesus said that it is the truth that sets us free. He is the Way, the Truth and the Life. We are sent to bring that Truth to all by faithfully living according to the teachings of the Church.

Pope John Paul II with the then Archbishop of Canterbury in 1982.

Activities

1. Match the beginnings and ends of the following sentences:

(a) The Church was founded by Jesus with...

(b) The Pope is...

(c) The Second Vatican Council...

(d) Other Christians respect the Pope...

(e) All Christians strive together to make...

...introduced major reforms.

...St. Peter as its leader.

...the world a better place.

...the direct successor of St. Peter.

...but do not accept him as leader of their Church.

2. Design a poster that shows how Christians of different denominations do work together for a better world.

3. Explain why the Catholic Church claims that it can trace its origin back to Jesus and the apostles.

97

The Church in Britain

Research

4. Write Chapter 5 of your history of the Church in Britain and give it the title: Life as a Catholic after Vatican II.

5. Interview one or two older people who are Catholics, for example, grandparents. Find out what changes they have seen in the Church in their lifetime. Or..

Interview one or two older people of another Christian Church. Find out which Church they belong to. Ask them if they have noticed any changes in the relationship between the different Churches in their lifetime. If the answer is 'yes', find out what they are.

Project

6. Work in Groups to share research material in order to complete your story of the Church in Britain.

Key Points to Remember

The Catholic Church alone makes a unique claim to be the one true Church established by Christ: "For it is through Christ's Catholic Church alone, which is the universal help towards salvation, that the fullness of salvation can be obtained". (Decree on Ecumenism)

Glossary

ADHERENTS - people who follow certain traditions or practices.

ADULTERY - to be unfaithful to one's husband or wife.

AGONY - extreme pain.

ALOES - juices from a Middle Eastern plant.

ANCESTORS - people of the same race who lived many years before.

ANNULMENT - declaration that a marriage is not valid, does not exist.

APOSTOLIC - descended directly from the apostles. Built on the foundation laid by the apostles and continuing their faith in the Risen Lord.

BITTER HERBS - some of the ingredients of the Passover Meal; ideally lettuce or parsley.

BLASPHEMY - claiming to be or insulting God.

BLESSED SACRAMENT - Christ's body, the consecrated host which is usually reserved (kept safe) in the tabernacle.

BOSOM - chest; it is used to mean "very close" to someone or intimate.

CALVARY - a hill outside the walls of Jerusalem where criminals were executed, also called 'Golgotha'.

CANONISE - when the Church recognises someone to be a saint.

CATHOLICS - Christians who believe in the universal Church; usually used to mean Roman Catholics (i.e. those who recogize the pope as their Head).

CATHOLIC SOCIAL TEACHING - what the Church has taught over the years on the subjects of justice and faithfulness.

CHALICE - the cup for the wine at Mass.

CHAMETZ - bread that contains yeast or grain.

CHRIST (THE) - the anointed one; the Messiah; God's chosen one.

COMPASSIONATE - caring, consideration.

CONCEPTION - the moment when a baby starts to form in its mother's womb.

CONSCIENCE - a person's understanding of what is right and what is wrong.

COVENANT - a solemn promise between two people or groups of people.

COVET - to have an unhealthy desire for something; to be jealous of someone else's possessions.

CREATION - when God made the universe - "the heavens and the earth".

DENIAL - claiming not to know someone or something.

Glossary

MYSTIC - a holy person who experiences visions.

NEGEB DESERT - a large area of bare land made up largely of rock and sand in southern Israel.

NEIGHBOUR - any other person, even someone we do not know particularly well.

NILE DELTA - the marshy area where the River Nile flows into the Mediterranean Sea.

OATH OF SUPREMACY - solemn acceptance that the king or queen is the Head of the Church in England.

PAGANS - people who believe in many gods rather than one God.

PASCHAL - related to the Passover

PASSION (THE) - the pain and suffering that Jesus experienced up to the moment of his death.

PASSOVER - originally, when God saved the Israelites from slavery in Egypt. Now celebrated at the 'Pesach' every Spring by the Jewish people.

PERSECUTE - to hunt down and punish people for their beliefs; to cause trouble and hurt to others.

PESACH - the annual Jewish festival of Passover.

PIETA - A statue of Mary holding the dead body of Jesus.

PRE-CREATION - when nothing at all existed - except God.

PRIEST HOLES - hiding places where priests were concealed to avoid arrest.

PROCLAIM - to speak out or to announce (important news).

PROCURATOR - another title for the Roman Governor.

PROPHECY - a message of divine truth revealing God's will; the act of speaking out such a message.

PROPHET - someone who proclaims God's messages; who speaks by divine inspiration.

PROTESTANT - a person who rejects (protests against) certain practices and beliefs in the Catholic Church.

PROTESTANTISM - a section of the Christian Church which rejects (protests against) certain practices and beliefs in the Catholic Church.

RED SEA - the waterway between Egypt and Israel (also known as the Reed Sea).

REFORMATION - the period in European history during which the Protestant Churches broke from the Catholic Church (16th Century).

REFUGEE - someone who flees their home or their country because it is unsafe to remain there.

Glossary

REMORSE - extreme sorrow and regret.

REPENT - to stop sinning, admit one's fault, ask for forgiveness from God and resolve not to sin again.

REVELATION - the way God showed himself to Israel by his Word; Christians believe that Jesus is God's full self-revelation.

ROMAN GOVERNOR - the senior Roman in an occupied territory; the Emperor's representative.

THE SABBATH - the day of rest/seventh day of the week (Saturday in the Jewish calendar, Sunday for Christians).

SALVATION - being completely close to God; being saved from our fallen state.

SANHEDRIN - the Jews' ruling council.

SAVIOUR - someone who frees people from hardships or slavery.

SCIENTIFIC TRUTHS - statements which can be proven scientifically.

SEDER - the special meal that is celebrated at Passover.

S.J. - initials which indicate that a priest belongs to the religious order called the Society of Jesus; he is a Jesuit.

SOFT LIES - what people want to hear.

SONS OF ISRAEL - the Israelites; descendants of Abraham.

SPICES - used in the treatment of a dead body.

SPIRITUAL - regarding matters of religion; the spirit, as opposed to the body.

SPOUSE - husband or wife.

STEWARD - a person whose task it is to look after something.

STEWARDSHIP - the task of looking after/caring for things.

SUPERSTITION - a belief in something magical or connected to the paranormal.

SUSTAINER - God, who keeps creation in existence.

SYMBOL - something that is used to help people understand difficult ideas.

SYMBOLIC - using a sign or story to explain something difficult.

SYNAGOGUE - place for Jewish prayer and learning.

SYNOD - a meeting of Church leaders where policies and important decisions are agreed.

TABERNACLE - a special receptacle, box, kind of safe in which the Blessed Sacrament is kept. It is to be found in a prominent place in the church, usually on an altar.

THE TEMPLE - the central place of worship and sacrifice for the Jews in Jerusalem.

Glossary

TEMPORAL - regarding matters of politics or society; to do with this world.

TEMPTER (THE) - the devil or evil one.

THEOLOGICAL TRUTHS - statements about God and his relationship with humans which cannot be proved scientifically but which are nonetheless believed to be true.

THIRD WORLD - Name given to the poor and developing countries.

TRADITION - knowledge, beliefs and customs that are handed down from one generation to the next. A doctrine believed as having been established by Christ or the apostles though not contained in Scripture.

TREASON - opposing and threatening the government or the leader of the State (emperor, king etc).

UNLEAVENED BREAD - bread made without yeast so it does not rise.

THE UPPER ROOM - where Jesus and his disciples celebrated the Last Supper, and where he appeared to them after his resurrection.

VIA DOLOROSA - the Way of Sorrows; the route that Jesus took to Calvary.

VIGIL - staying awake, often during the night before a big event.

VISION - a supernatural revelation.

WILDERNESS - a bleak land, desert.

WOE - intense grief, affliction, misfortune.

YEAST - the ingredient that is added to dough to make it rise, to make bread.

YOKE - a harness sometimes used on oxen or for carrying something heavy.